M000197651

THY KINGDOM COME

THY KINGDOM COME

Living the Lord's Prayer in Everyday Life

Fr. Jeffrey Kirby, STD

TAN Books

Gastonia, North Carolina

Thy Kingdom Come: Living the Lord's Prayer in Everyday Life ©
2019 Jeffrey Kirby

All rights reserved. With the exception of short excerpts used
in critical review, no part of this work may be reproduced,
transmitted, or stored in any form whatsoever, without the
prior written permission of the publisher.

Unless otherwise noted, Scripture quotations are from the
Revised Standard Version of the Bible—Second Catholic
Edition (Ignatius Edition), copyright © 2006 National
Council of the Churches of Christ in the United States of
America. Used by permission. All rights reserved.

Excerpts from the English translation of the Catechism of
the Catholic Church for use in the United States of America
© 1994, United States Catholic Conference, Inc.—Libreria
Editrice Vaticana. Used with permission.

Cover design by Caroline Green

Library of Congress Control Number: 2019957920

ISBN: 978-1-5051-1584-0

Published in the United States by
TAN Books
PO Box 269
Gastonia, NC 28053
www.TANBooks.com

Printed in the United States of America

To
My Father,
Alan Joseph Kirby, Jr.

Praise for *Thy Kingdom Come* . . .

Fr. Kirby offers solid and practical guidance for contemplating and living each of the seven petitions of the Lord's Prayer. Along the way, he helps us to discover how to draw closer to God through the Beatitudes, virtues, gifts of the Spirit etc. His exciting "school of discipleship" is all about making deep connections. Highly recommended!

—SCOTT HAHN, PHD
Fr. Michael Scanlan Chair of Biblical Theology and the New Evangelization, Franciscan University of Steubenville

The "Our Father" is so ingrained in the minds of most Christians that we all too often recite it merely by rote. *Thy Kingdom Come* is a most welcome reminder of the worlds of meaning in every phrase of the prayer that Jesus taught us.

—MARY ANN GLENDON
Former U.S. Ambassador to the Holy See

Clearly, Fr. Jeff Kirby has reflected deeply on the words of Lord's Prayer. In this book, he shares his insights to help us experience more fully the love of the heart of our heavenly Father.

—FATHER MICHAEL GAITLEY, MIC
Author of *33 Days to Merciful Love*

CONTENTS

FOREWORD

The early Church writer Tertullian made the striking comment that the Lord's Prayer "is truly the summary of the whole gospel." And he went on to say, "In summaries of so few words, how many utterances of the prophets, the Gospels, the apostles—how many discourses, examples, parables of the Lord, are touched on! How many duties are simultaneously discharged!" In its explanation of this summary of the Gospel, *Thy Kingdom Come* provides us with rich fare, drawing out the words of the Our Father and demonstrating how the gifts of the Holy Spirit, the Beatitudes, and the virtues unite around its petitions—and also how the individual petitions strengthen us against the vices and sins that threaten to dislodge the work of God within us.

The Our Father is a prayer. Father Kirby draws out for us here its riches as a *teaching* from the Lord. Well-known for his ability to unite vibrant and engaging teaching with a deep concern for building up the spiritual life, he provides in this latest work sustenance for our Christian lives through a wholesome diet of good teaching. This work not only feeds the mind but also draws out and strengthens the heart at the same time. Here we will find strong foundations for sustaining our response to the Lord's invitation to us.

The Our Father offers us doctrine in the form of prayer. It provides us with the center and heart of what we can term a "dogmatic spirituality." There are many spiritualities in the Church's tradition—Franciscan, Dominican, Ignatian, Carmelite, and so on. Each one of these offers a distinct path, a distinct way of living out the call to holiness. However, underlying each of these paths and structuring them in different ways are the central truths of the faith that are the fundamental bedrock of our lives. The magnificent truths concerning the Blessed Trinity, concerning Jesus Christ, true God and true man, concerning our participation in the life of grace—it is from these that we live, and from which we draw our deepest springs of life. And these truths and the Christian way that flows from them is summed up for us in this prayer taught to us by Our Lord. Here we have the "quintessential" prayer of the *whole* Church (CCC 2776), the prayer common to *all* Christian paths and spiritualities, the prayer that sums up the Gospel.

This work by Father Kirby uses the same catechetical approach towards the Lord's Prayer as is found in his recent book on the Beatitudes. As with that work, this new publication not only teaches but also explores the depth and *practical* application of what St. Thomas Aquinas described as "the most perfect of prayers." The subtitle to Father Kirby's work provides us with his key focus: "*Living the Lord's Prayer in Everyday Life.*" The beautiful uniting of narrative and personal witness that we find here, together with an evident pastoral wisdom and a penetrating examination of conscience attached to each petition, enable us to see how the words of this prayer can truly "take flesh" in in our lives.

And throughout this overriding concern for the *living* of

the prayer, Father Kirby never lets us forget that the growth of the kingdom of God in life is itself a thing unseen and secret. The source of its growth consists precisely in the relationship of prayer and in the love and service of God growing in our hearts. For each of us, he provides a reminder here of the priority that the Church has always accorded to prayer and to contemplation, where we find "a communion of love bearing Life for the multitude" (CCC 2719). While Father Kirby helps us to look outwards from prayer into life, he also helps us to remember that our outward gaze of love flows from the fact that the Father has first looked upon us with love in secret.

The Scottish poet Edwin Muir captures the essence of such a gaze, coming from the eyes of Love into ordinary life, beautifully in his poem *Annunciation*:

> The angel and the girl are met. . . .
> See, they have come together, see,
> While the destroying minutes flow,
> Each reflects the other's face
> Till heaven in hers and earth in his
> Shine steadily there . . .
>
> Outside the window footsteps fall
> Into the ordinary day
> And with the sun along the wall
> Pursue their unreturning way . . .
>
> But through the endless afternoon
> These neither speak nor movement make,
> But stare into their deepening trance
> As if their gaze would never break.

It is the power of just such a gaze, the gaze of the Father, that this most perfect of prayers gives to us if we are faithful to it, and which allows us to turn towards others in everyday life.

Petroc Willey STL, PhD
Director of the Office of Catechetics and the
Catechetical Institute
Franciscan University of Steubenville

PREFACE

New Awareness

Thank you for picking up this book!

Many of us know the words of the Lord's Prayer, often learning them as we were still learning to speak. We assume we know what these words mean, but their depth can be taken for granted. This book is designed to get us beyond what we think we know and instead guide us through the beauty and wisdom of the prayer. It's also meant to show us the practical dimensions and applications of the prayer.

"Our Father"

Some years ago, my brother traveled with me to a parish mission in Florida. When we arrived, the local parish leaders invited us out to dinner. We were happy to join them. The group was a happy bunch. The food was good, the conversation was pleasant, and there was an overall sense of welcome and joy.

At some point in the meal, one of the parish leaders asked my brother and me a question about our family. While attempting to answer her question, I said something like, "Well, *our father* was in the military. . . ." I stopped and chuckled. The words *our father* were so close to the opening words of the Lord's Prayer that they struck me and sounded comical. The wording was unique for me.

Normally, I would travel by myself or with an assistant who is not a family member. Or, if I *was* with my brother or sister, I would use the more colloquial "Dad." Or, many times, I would use a singular pronoun, "my father," with the presumption that it extended to one of my siblings. For all these reasons, I was surprised by my use of "*our father.*"

Later, as I thought about it, I realized that there are only two people on the entire planet with whom I could use that term—namely, my brother and my sister. We three are the children of one father. We are united by one father. And only with one another can we use the plural pronoun *our.* This reflection helped me grasp the closeness I have with my brother and sister *because of my father.* It helped me to feel even more loved and more united with my father, my siblings, and my family.

This brief story illustrates what the Lord Jesus says and offers to each of us. As he led the apostles in their tutorial on prayer, Jesus said, "Our Father." He united himself to each of us as a true sibling. He draws familial bonds with us and reveals the Father to us. The Lord says to us, "Yes, he is *our Father.* I say this with you because we are the children of the same Father. What I am by nature, you are by adoption. We are united. We are family. We are given a kingdom and a way of life. Accept the Father's love. Live in that love. Share his message. Spread this kingdom."

Some Helpful Truths

For this reason, the Lord entrusted us with his prayer. The words of the prayer can teach and form our hearts to have the interior attitude of Jesus. It can show us the relationship that the Lord has with God the Father by the power of the Holy Spirit. As we seek to imitate this relationship in our own lives, we think, love, and act more and more as the children of God. This book will explore this inner rapport and display for us the internal outline and way of life that are a part of being a beloved child of God.

As a start, here's some good news drawn from the Lord's Prayer.

You Are Greatly Loved

Our fallen world tells us that we need to earn love. We have to look or conform to a certain way of life that is merely external or self-centered if we want to be loved. Love has been redefined as pleasure or as a person's own emotional fulfillment, or as manipulation or control over the freedom of others. With such fragmented views of love, many people have given up on the idea of true and lasting love. Many people do not trust love and they recoil at the very idea. But God smashes the idols of false love and breaks through the façade of false definitions, and in his Son, Jesus Christ, he declares an everlasting love for each of us. He says to us what he said to the Lord Jesus, "This is my beloved Son, with whom I am well pleased" (Mt 3:17).

God invites us to live boldly and to accept this amazing offer of true love. He can tear down the barriers of narcissism and misguided love and offer a true relationship because he is Love (cf. 1 Jn 4:7–21). And authentic love is seeking the good of another (cf. Jn 15:13; 1 Jn 3:16). We are told by St. Paul, "Love is patient and kind; love is not jealous or boastful; it is not arrogant or rude. Love does not insist on its way; it is not irritable or resentful; it does not rejoice at wrong, but rejoices in the right. Love bears all things, hopes all things, endures all things. Love never ends" (1 Cor 13:4–8). This is who God is, and it's the life-giving love that he offers to each of us.

You Have a Loving Father

The love that God has for each of us reaches its fullest expression in one word: *father*. This word summarizes the fullness of concern, care, acceptance, affection, protection, affirmation, discipline, and selfless service that we all crave as human beings and need in order to flourish as children of God (cf. Heb 12:3–11). It's important to stress this heavenly standard. When we call God "Father," we are not projecting a human relationship onto God. Quite the contrary! Any man who has been given the vocation of fatherhood is merely imitating the same role God fulfills over the whole of humanity (cf. Eph 3:15).

God is not like a human father. God is Father. His entire being is Father. And certain men on earth are blessed with this title since their vocation is to reflect God in their families. These men are given a divine title. Sadly, we know not every man lives up to this vocation (or even tries to live up to it). This neglect or brokenness can cause great harm to their children and families. Perhaps you've suffered through this brokenness. The good news is that no matter what our earthly experience has been of our fathers, we all have a loving and caring heavenly Father (cf. Mt 7:11).

This Father was fully revealed to us by Jesus Christ (cf. Mt 11:25–27), and God greatly desires to be this Father to you, to me, and to each of his beloved children. He wants to heal any wounds, console any pain, and bless us with the hope and strength that comes with his love.

You Are Called to Be a Member of God's Family

As human beings, we are hardwired for community and need acceptance, love, and belonging. We were made that way since we were created in the image of the living God (Gn 1:27). And God is not eternal solitude! The living God dwells forever as a divine family: the Father, Son, and Holy Spirit (cf. Jn 17:1–5; Mt 28:19–20). We were created in the image of this divine family, planting an innate impulse within each of us to search for the living God and worship him, and to share divine fellowship with him. This is also why we have an inescapable drive in our human nature to have family ties and to be in a community with other people.

God searches for us, he calls to us, and invites us to be a part of his divine family. He sent his Son, Jesus Christ, to ransom us from the darkness of our fallen world, and in his saving work, the Lord Jesus revealed the face of our Father to us. Jesus wants to show us the way to the Father. In our sinfulness, we want to make God a harsh judge or cruel master. We want to see ourselves as slaves, as if God is repressing us or destroying our freedom. It's as if he wants us to fear him, or so we think. This master/slave paradigm is completely dismantled by the teachings of Jesus Christ. He unveils that God is a loving Father and we are called to be in his family. God wants a Father/child relationship with us. He wants us to flourish, grow, and prosper as his children.

In this way, we can say that the single word *father* is a summary of the entire plan of salvation. It discloses the very heart of God and the identity from which he loves and to which he calls us.

Jesus shows us the way to join God's family. When the apostles asked Jesus to teach them how to pray (Mt 6:9), he told them, "Pray then like this: Our Father . . ." Did you catch that pronoun? He said "our." He included us with himself. The Son sees us as his brothers and siblings by grace. God is Father to us all and Jesus, who is Lord, is also our older brother. He is the firstborn of all creation (cf. Col 1:15–20). We are invited to be a part of this family. The Lord welcomes us into the divine family. This is the reason why we were made and is the only source of complete happiness.

God's Family Is a Kingdom

When we accept the invitation to be a part of God's family, we also enter a kingdom. It's a kingdom of truth, love, justice, peace, and reconciliation. Living as members of this kingdom, we're formed and educated on what we should desire in our hearts, and even the process, or sequence, in which they should be desired. This path is shown to us the more we say yes to God's will and the more we desire his will over our own.

You Are Commissioned to Spread This Kingdom

When we see the goodness of God's kingdom, we begin to realize its power. We deepen in our commitment that God's kingdom can bring light from darkness, healing from brokenness, and grace from sinfulness. This causes a deep desire within us to spread God's kingdom and to see it manifested in our world. As the children of God, we grow in our commission to announce, labor, and suffer for his kingdom. The more we realize the glory that is offered to us, the more we pine and groan for God's kingdom to triumph. This is the kingdom entrusted to us, and as the children of God, we determine if, where, and how it will come.

In going through all of these points, you might be struck by the depth and breadth of the truths. And it might cause you to ask, "Are all these really contained in one prayer?" The definitive answer is yes, all of these truths are contained, taught, and proclaimed in the Lord's Prayer.

This book will help us journey through these different truths and understand everything that the Lord Jesus wants to show us.

Diving Deeper

In reviewing these essential points from the Lord's Prayer, you have taken the first step. But there is so much more! We need to begin a deeper exploration of the seven principal tenets of the prayer entrusted to us by Jesus Christ, who is God and man, Lord and older brother. I invite you to take this deeper dive and continue reading as we dissect and evaluate each portion of this sacred prayer.

The Lord prays, "Thy kingdom come." Let this same petition be in our hearts. Let it inspire us to dive deeper!

THE TALE OF TWO FATHERS

Jesus said to them, "If God were your Father, you would love me, for I proceeded and came forth from God; I came not of my own accord, but he sent me. Why do you not understand what I say? It is because you cannot bear to hear my word. You are of your father the devil, and your will is to do your father's desires. He was a murderer from the beginning, and has nothing to do with the truth, because there is no truth in him. When he lies, he speaks according to his own nature, for he is a liar and the father of lies."

JOHN 8:42–44

A Father's Witness

Many years ago, my older brother was deployed to Afghanistan. He was born to be a soldier, jumping out of perfectly good airplanes and eagerly running into situations that most people flee. And yet, this deployment was heavy on everyone's heart. The situation in the war-torn area at the time would come to be seen as one of the worst in the decades-long military

1

engagement. As the time came for my brother's departure, he was unusually nervous. My mother was crying and my father seemed extraordinarily pensive.

As my brother prepared to leave, my father gave the softly spoken command, "Stop," and that was enough to suspend our world. As a retired soldier, dad always spoke succinctly and one pitch above what most people would consider normal. The muffled, one-word order seemed to stop everything. We all looked. We all waited.

From his pocket, my father pulled out a small golden lock. It looked like something that would be used to lock a small file cabinet. I hadn't seen it before. He showed it to the family and then specifically to my brother. He took my brother by the shoulder and walked him over to the grandfather clock that was always in the living room. It was an anniversary gift from my father to my mother many years before. The clock was as much a fixture in the house as us kids. As Dad walked my brother over to the clock, we all followed. It became a quiet little procession for a family that's usually loud and all over the place.

When my dad got to the grandfather clock, he took the lock from his hand, reached out, and locked it on the door. As he did this, he was visibly shaking and holding back tears. After closing the lock, he turned to my brother and with a sadness that only love can understand, said to him, "This is where my heart will be until you come home."

It was a rare disclosure of the tender love that fills my father's heart and that constantly seeks to care for and protect his children and family. While it was usually expressed in hard work, sacrifice, and tempered discipline, my father's love was tangible in that single, sacred moment. For my dad, the lock was his heart and the grandfather clock was the time that my brother would be away at war.

Throughout his deployment, every delay in communication with my brother set my father into distant thought. He would regularly rub his hands and was slow to laugh. And every time there was an email, or letter, or even a phone call from my brother, Dad was elated and on cloud nine for days. In many respects, my father absorbed and expressed the emotions of the entire family.

It was a joy for all of us when my brother came home. I will never forget how my father embraced him and the tears he shed that day. As I will also never forget walking into the living room the next day and seeing the golden lock removed and gone from the grandfather clock.

This story illustrates one father's intense love and sense of mission for his family. It's a story that's played out in various ways and with different details in families throughout the world. It's called fatherhood. And as moving and inspiring as some of the stories are about our earthly fathers, they are mere reflections of the all-holy love and affection that God the Father has for each one of us.

As we see shining examples of fatherhood in this world, we are invited to look above and to realize that these men, called to be fathers on earth, are reflections and witnesses of our eternal Father who dwells in unending light. We are called to see God's love for us and to acknowledge and accept his perfect fatherhood into our lives. Each of us is welcomed into his family. We are invited to hear the tender words of the Lord Jesus, "*Our Father,*" and to make them our own. We are offered the grace to live as members of God's family, and not as some lost orphans or abandoned children.

We have a choice. We have a heavenly Father who loves us and who wants to care for and protect us in the midst of a fallen and broken world that can hurt and harm us. In the midst of it all, our Father beckons to us. He calls us by name. Will we accept?

Two Families, Two Fathers, Two Kingdoms

The invitation given to us by God our Father to accept and reciprocate his love is fully developed in the Lord's Prayer. Throughout the tenets of this great prayer, the tender care and affection God has for each of us is on complete display. In this systematic way, we can clearly see throughout the prayer how deeply God loves us and wants to bless us.

But we know there's another offer on the table. Made free, we have a choice. And there is a false father—a liar—who wants us to follow him in his narcissism and rebellion against God.

In the options given to us, we have two families, two fathers:

- There is the divine family—the Father, the Son, and the Holy Spirit—with the fatherhood of the living God.

Or

- There is the infinitely inferior, fallen family—me, myself, and I—with the deceptive, selfish fatherhood of the evil one.

These two families, and these two fathers, are placed before us. We have to decide which of the two families we will have fellowship with, which of the two fathers we will have father us, and which of the two kingdoms we will spread in our world.

Before his passion, death, and resurrection, the Lord Jesus solemnly promised us, "I will not leave you desolate; I will come to you. Yet a little while, and the world will see me no more, but you will see me; because I live, you will live also. In that day you will know that I am in my Father, and you in me, and I in you. He who has my commandments and keeps them, he it is who loves me; and he who loves me will be loved by my Father, and I will love him and manifest myself to him" (Jn 14:18–21).

In this promise, the Christ—who conquers evil and dispels darkness—tells us that those who love him and keep his commands will not be orphans. When he accomplishes his saving work and departs, those who obey him will be "in him" and dwell with the Father. The Lord also tells his followers that he will send the Spirit to guide them. The conditional aspect of this promise cannot be overlooked or taken for granted. The Lord indicated that the divine family, and the blessings that come with divine fellowship, will be given to those who love him and obey him. In short, the graces will be given to those who truly want them.

The evil one, who is also called the devil (which means "accuser") or Satan (which means "adversary"), offers us an easier life. The fellowship he offers has no blessing but is consumed with egotism, power, vanity, wealth, and pleasure. It calls for no obedience other than to one's own whims and fantasies. It's a glamorous offer, the spiritual equivalent of flashing lights, loud music, and egocentric celebrations. Rather than love of God and neighbor, we are offered a life of conceit and self-absorption.

These are two ways of life flowing from two families, two fathers, and two kingdoms. The choice is ours. What will we decide?

Internal Structure of the Lord's Prayer

The Lord's Prayer contains a spiritual portrait of Jesus's entire life. He reveals how we are to live as a son or daughter of God. Whenever we pray it, therefore, we should always remember that we pray it through, with, and in Jesus. In Jesus Christ, the prayer provides us with an interior path for us to follow. The path described in the prayer provides us with seven tenets, or signposts, along the way.

After the earth-shaking salutation, "Our Father," the prayer moves into a three-fold declaration of praise and a four-fold series of petitions. The two portions of the prayer reflect the two tablets of the Ten Commandments: the first pertains to our adoration of God, while the second pertains to what we need from God and how we are to interact with our neighbor.

The first portion of the Lord's Prayer consists of his glory: "Thy Name," "Thy Kingdom," and "Thy Will."

The second portion of the Lord's Prayer consists of our poverty: "Give us," "Forgive us," "Lead us," and "Deliver us."

As we can see, the Lord's Prayer teaches us to realize what we should desire and guides us to recognize the sequence in which things should be desired. This book will walk through the sequence, describing each tenet, and developing what each one means and how we can understand and use them in our search and struggle to live as the children of God.

"School of Discipleship"

In moving forward, we'll explore the salutation of the prayer. After the salutation, we'll walk through each tenet of the Lord's Prayer, showing how it's lived out in Scripture and in everyday life, as well as examine their amazing connections to the Beatitudes, the Gifts of the Holy Spirit, the virtues of the Christian tradition, and the deadly sins.

At the close of each chapter on the various tenets of the prayer, you will see a kind of "spiritual matrix" unfold before your eyes, found in a section called "School of Discipleship." This matrix, or chart, outlines a web of connections that link the central components of our spiritual life. For the purposes of our "School of Discipleship," we will call these "Subjects." Only the row in question can be found in each chapter, but the complete matrix can be seen in the back.

If you have read my book from 2018, *Kingdom of Happiness*, then this "School" should sound familiar. This spiritual matrix was first used as a platform for a discussion of the Beatitudes, while in this book our focus is the Lord's Prayer. If you have not read *Kingdom of Happiness*, I encourage you to go read it after this book. The books are not written in any specific order but rather show the beautiful harmony that exists between all these aspects of the spiritual life.

To help you better understand these "Subjects," here is a brief description of each one. Please read these summaries now and refer back to them, if needed, as you read through the book.

Beatitudes: The *Catechism of the Catholic Church* calls the Beatitudes "the heart of Jesus' preaching" (CCC 1716) and identifies them as "the countenance of Jesus Christ" (CCC

1717).The Beatitudes are further described as expressing "the vocation of the faithful associated with the glory of his Passion and Resurrection; they shed light on the actions and attitudes characteristic of the Christian life; they are the paradoxical promises that sustain hope in the midst of tribulations" (CCC 1717). In the twists and turns of life, the Beatitudes are the quick reference points of the kingdom of God. The *Catechism* teaches us that "the Beatitudes confront us with decisive choices concerning earthly goods; they purify our hearts in order to teach us to love God above all things" (CCC 1728).

Christian Virtues: The *Catechism* defines virtue as "an habitual and firm disposition to do good. It allows the person not only to perform good acts, but to give the best of himself. The virtuous person tends toward the good with all his sensory and spiritual powers; he pursues the good and chooses it in concrete actions" (CCC 1803). St. Gregory of Nyssa, in his *On the Beatitudes,* says, "The goal of a virtuous life is to become like God." The *Catechism* names seven Christian, or "heavenly," virtues, broken up into two categories. The four cardinal virtues are prudence, justice, temperance, and courage, while the three theological virtues are faith, hope, and charity (see CCC 1804–29).

Gifts of the Holy Spirit: The *Catechism* tells us that "the moral life of Christians is sustained by the gifts of the Holy Spirit. These are permanent dispositions which make man docile in following the promptings of the Holy Spirit. . . . They belong in their fullness to Christ, Son of David. They complete and perfect the virtues of those who receive them" (CCC 1830–31). In short, these are exactly what they sound like—generous gifts from the Third Person of the Holy Trinity, which he bestows upon us at the will of the Father.

They allow us to become better and more virtuous people and overcome the pitfalls of the deadly sins. The seven gifts of the Holy Spirit are wisdom, understanding, counsel, fortitude, knowledge, piety, and fear of the Lord (sometimes referred to as "wonder" or "awe").

Seven Deadly Sins: The *Catechism* defines sin as "an offense against reason, truth, and right conscience; it is failure in genuine love for God and neighbor caused by a perverse attachment to certain goods. It wounds the nature of man and injures human solidarity" (CCC 1849). Though there are many different sorts of sins, the Church and her tradition classifies them in a list of seven "capital" or "deadly" sins. Each transgression we commit can be traced back to pride, avarice (greed), envy, wrath, lust, gluttony, and sloth (CCC 1866).

Note: As you read through the explanation and study the chart, remember that we are drawing all these things back to the tenets of the Lord's Prayer, not necessarily drawing parallels between the "Subjects" themselves. While the Christian tradition does have a history of showing the interconnectedness of these aspects of the spiritual life, our work is focused on their relationship to the Lord's Prayer. Additionally, all explanations are kept brief to simply graze the surface of this rich theology. For any reader who wishes to go deeper, see the bibliography for resources that can provide more detail.

CHAPTER I

THE SALUTATION

Our Father who art in heaven.

MATTHEW 6:9

Our Father, Who Art in Heaven

The Lord's Prayer begins with the bold salutation: "Our Father who art in heaven." At every Mass, we are reminded of this boldness when the priest prefaces the prayer by saying, "At the Savior's command and formed by divine teaching, *we dare to say . . .*"

It is indeed bold to call God our Father; that is why we "dare" to call him this. Who are we, poor sinners, to call him Father? And yet the Lord Jesus affirms this boldness. In giving us this prayer, he uses the plural pronoun *our*, and so indicates that we are together with him in God's family. As the Lord is the Son of God by nature, so we become sons and daughters of God by grace. As adopted sons and daughters, we are also siblings to the Lord Jesus and so heirs with him in glory (cf. Rom 8:14–17).

As we pray with Jesus and hail "Our Father," we also

announce that our Father dwells in heaven. This declaration is both an assertion of God's sovereignty—he is All-Holy—as well as of our belonging—he calls us to be with him in heaven forever.

Truly, God lives in the abode of glory, far above us in majesty, but his home is also our eternal home as he walks with us and calls us to be with him. And so, when we pray that God dwells in heaven, we are reminding ourselves of our final end and of our everlasting homeland.

Our True Home

There was once a husband and wife who were both missionaries. The two went to the missions in Africa early in their marriage. They spent most of their lives sharing the Gospel and serving the poor and sick. They started their family in the missions, raised their children in the missions, and grew old in the missions. Upon entering their later years, they returned to their homeland for needed medical attention and a much-earned retirement.

As things turned out, the two missionaries were on the same flight home as a noted diplomat and author. When the plane landed, there was immense fanfare for the distinguished person. There was a small band, balloons, banners, and an eager waiting party. All the passengers were held on the plane while the diplomat-author was allowed to triumphantly exit to the sound of music and applause. As this was going on, the two missionaries waited patiently in their seats.

After the fanfare and the approval from the cockpit, other passengers began to rummage through the overhead compartments and rush to get off the plane. The missionaries were not accustomed to the process and sat quietly in their seats. After most of the passengers had departed from the plane, the couple found their simple belongings and moved toward the exit. By the time they reached the stairway at the plane's door, they saw balloons being popped, banners being brought down, musicians loading up their instruments, and an empty runway.

The missionaries made their way into the airport, and as they got their bearings, it was clear that the wife had a heavy heart. She turned to her husband and with a whispered and crackling voice, said to him, "Did you see that ceremony? So much pomp. You know, after so many decades away in service to so many, I thought there might be a little something, even something small, waiting for us when we finally came home. The woman's husband, turning to her with understanding but also with a smile, said, "Oh, honey, just wait. We're not home yet!"

The husband was stating an awesome truth. Heaven awaits those who love God. And St. Paul reminds us, "What no eye has seen, nor ear heard, nor the heart of man conceived, what God has prepared for those who love him" (1 Cor 2:9).

This is the reality of heaven!

As every family has a father, so every family has a home. Our Father is the Ancient of Days, the All-Holy One, and our home is heaven. Heaven is the presence of our Father, who dwells in majestic light, eternal majesty, and infinite glory. It is our true homeland, and our Father "who art in heaven" calls us to be with him. Our life on earth is a time of blessing and preparation. It is the path that can lead us to accept our Father's invitation and to dwell with him in the everlasting joys of heaven.

This understanding raises two questions in our hearts: Who is this Father God who loves us so much? What is this homeland where he lives in such glory?

Our Father

Some people believe that as human beings we are projecting our societal conditions and familial roles onto God. The argument goes something like this: God is greater than any of our human titles and roles. We have forced these upon God. This has hurt our approach to God and our society. It would be better for us if we just stopped using these outdated structures altogether, stopped applying them to God, and approached God on our own terms and let "God be God."

This view is particularly applied to fatherhood since it's argued that so many people have been hurt or abused by their earthly fathers and the title is no longer helpful to anyone. It's asserted that fatherhood is an antiquated role that is best left in the past.

That's heavy, and there's a lot to unpack there. But once we dissect some of these statements, we'll be able to come to an even greater awareness of what it means to have God as our true Father. Here are some helpful clarifications.

The Eternal God lives forever as *Father*. This is not a metaphor or symbol. This is not a title that we invented or that we impose upon him. In the infinitely perfect life of the Most Holy Trinity, the First Person is, has always been, and will always be *Father*. The All-Powerful One and the All-Compassionate One has revealed himself to us as Father. The power he holds is synonymous with his paternity. He is Father just as he is Love. He has freely chosen to give us this intimate disclosure of himself as father and so unveil himself to us as he truly is. It's important for us to put first things first and to acknowledge what has always come first: God is Father. We are not forcing him into any human standard or social construct. God dwells forever as Father.

Throughout the Bible, this fatherhood of God is described in many ways. On one occasion, the prophet Hosea gives this powerful and tender account of God teaching and caring for a young Israel:

> When Israel was a child, I loved him,
> and out of Egypt I called my son.
> The more I called them,
> the more they went from me;
> they kept sacrificing to the Baals,
> and offering incense to idols.
>
> Yet it was I who taught Ephraim to walk,
> I took them up in my arms;
> but they did not know that I healed them.
> I led them with cords of compassion,
> with bands of love,
> and became to them as one
> who raises an infant to his cheeks,
> and I bent down to them and fed them. . . .
>
> How can I give you up, O Ephraim?
> How can I hand you over, O Israel? . . .
> My heart recoils within me;
> my compassion grows warm and tender. (Hos
> 11:1–4, 8)

Throughout the course of history, from Adam to our present day, God has chosen to share his very fatherhood with certain men in the human family. He has selected specific men, empowered them, and given them the grace to reflect his own fatherhood in their respective families. It is the human father who has been given a divine gift rather than God who is being forced into a human construct. St. Paul tells us that every family receives its name from the heavens (cf. Eph 3:15). In similar fashion, every father receives his fatherhood from the Eternal Father. The selected man is even blessed with the very name of God, as his children call him "father."

It is vital for human fathers, therefore, to realize that they have been marked as witnesses to God our Father. They are summoned to selflessly accept this vocation that God has given them and to labor throughout their lives to fulfill its responsibilities in a loving and virtuous way.

With these explanations, we can now see fatherhood in a rightly ordered way, *from the heavens to the earth*. We can realize that the best way we "let God be God" is by accepting his own revelation of himself—namely, to accept the revelation that God is forever Father.

Our invitation, therefore, is to receive this revelation and to embrace God's fatherhood in our lives. Will we "let God be God" and accept him as he truly is? Will we allow God to be true Father to us?

Fatherhood in "Earthen Vessels"

The divine and proper ordering of fatherhood is very important. Rather than starting from our human experience and working up to God, we're able to redirect our focus. We

rightly start with God and work to see things from his perspective. In this way, we can place the faults and the hurts
caused by human fathers within a broader context, allowing
for exhortation, affirmation, correction, and healing.

Admittedly, the men who are called to be fathers are
found across the spectrum of temperament, personality, abilities, and virtue. Although fallen themselves, most earthly
fathers do their best to love and care for their children. As St.
Paul reminds us of all heavenly gifts: "But we have this treasure in earthen vessels, that the excellency of the power may
be of God, and not of us" (1 Cor 4:7).

Yes, the gift of fatherhood is given to weak men. They hold
this heavenly treasure in "earthen vessels"—namely, in their
own brokenness and sinfulness. Even the best of fathers will
sometimes get distracted, make mistakes, and forgo the glory
that has been entrusted to them. This is why, at every turn,
men-turned-fathers are beckoned by God to pay attention,
to do their best, and to always fight the good fight seeking to
be true ambassadors on earth of our Father in heaven (cf. 2
Tm 4:7; 2 Cor 5:20).

Unfortunately, and to the great suffering of their children,
there are some fathers who willingly and habitually neglect or
offend their children. Some even hurt and abuse their children.
These are the group of fathers who sacrilege the vocation of
fatherhood that God has given to them. They cause reser-
vation and suspicion in the hearts of their children toward
fatherhood. Rather than fatherhood being seen as a source
of stability, education, love, and selfless service—reflecting
God our Father—fatherhood instead becomes a place of fear,
delinquency, deceit and maltreatment. Such harm leaves scars
and memories that are hard to heal.

In recognizing God as our Father, however, we are able to see beyond our earthly fathers and whatever hurt or harm they may have caused us. We are able to behold what true fatherhood is and what it looks like when it's authentically lived out. And so, instead of fatherhood being a human construct forced on God and used by violent men to perpetuate darkness, we are able to comprehend fatherhood as a divine identity given to certain men, some of whom violate its holiness, but the vocation of fatherhood itself remains inherently good and noble since it has its origin and fulfillment in God himself.

This clarification can be a tremendous help to people who have suffered through negligent or hurtful earthly fathers. The truth of God's fatherhood can free a person from dark memories and heal painful wounds from the past.

God is Father and he wants us—his children—to know him. He wants us to know that fatherhood is about tender love and protective care, not iniquity and indifference.

With this perspective in mind, we can ask: What, then, are the attributes of true fatherhood? What does it look like? How do good earthly fathers model it for us?

True Fatherhood

The Sacred Scriptures go to great length to describe a good father. Each of these attributes give us a glimpse into the fatherhood of God. Before diving into specific traits, however, we can summarize the biblical notion of fatherhood as a supreme vocation to love prudently and selflessly. And a father's love, according to divine wisdom, is expressed in how he protects, cares for, feeds, provides for, and teaches his children. In particular, a father's instruction is focused on truth, virtue, discipline, and hard work (cf. Gn 18:19; Prv 4:1–9; Heb 12:4–13; 3 Jn 1:4).

Here is some wisdom from the Bible that illustrates these points:

> Look at the birds of the air: they neither sow nor reap nor gather into barns, and yet your heavenly Father feeds them. Are you not of more value than they? (Mt 6:26)

> Or what man of you, if his son asks him for bread, will give him a stone? Or if he asks for a fish, will give him a serpent? If you then, who are evil, know how to give good gifts to your children, how much more will your Father who is in heaven give good things to those who ask him! (Mt 7:9–11)

> For you know how, like a father with his children, we exhorted each one of you and encouraged you and charged you to walk in a manner worthy of God, who calls you into his own kingdom and glory. (1 Thes 2:11–12)

In breaking down this general summary, the Bible teaches us that a father must always view his children as a blessing, especially in moments of anger or disappointment (cf. Ps 127:3–5; Prv 19:18; Col 3:21). He is called to be a paradigm of righteousness and a model of both justice and mercy (cf. Prv 20:7). In addition, a father is summoned to hold virtuous and high standards for his children and provide them with the earthly and spiritual means to achieve them. He must be

tender but also exercise discipline (cf. Prv 13:24; Heb 12:7).
In this process, a father must exude unrelenting confidence
in his children. He is to manifest an overflowing compassion
towards them as they struggle to be virtuous and excellent in
all their tasks. He must be present and available when they fail
and need tough love or encouragement to help them get back
on track (cf. Dt 6:6–7; Ps 103:13).

In teaching his children about the ways of goodness, hard
work, and perseverance, a father's mission is to prepare his
children for lifelong virtue and success (cf. Prv 22:6; 23:24).
The Bible gives this testimony:

> He established a testimony in Jacob,
> and appointed a law in Israel,
> which he commanded our fathers
> to teach to their children;
> that the next generation might know them,
> the children yet unborn,
> and arise and tell them to their children,
> so that they should set their hope in God,
> but keep his commandments;
> and that they should not be like their fathers,
> a stubborn and rebellious generation,
> a generation whose heart was not steadfast,
> whose spirit was not faithful to God. (Ps 78:5–8)

In particular, the Bible calls on fathers to be motivating, accessible, and always ready to affirm and discipline their children
when they succeed or fail, prosper or suffer (cf. Prv 3:11–12;
Eph 6:4). A father's love must be constant and unconditional.
He is to be a foundation for his children that never wavers or
cracks.

In addition, a father instructs his children on righteous suffering and selfless service. He dies to himself by loving his wife without deference to himself or his desires, as Christ loves the Church (cf. Eph 3:15). A man's children witness this generous love to their mother. They also experience this same sacrificial love towards themselves as their father loves and cares for them.

A father also teaches his children, especially his sons, about fortitude and charitable service to the widow, orphan, and other vulnerable people (cf. Ps 68:5–6). A true father extends his paternity to the common good. He is attentive to the moves of culture and fights against any attack against the innocent or weak, especially children.

These are some of the prominent biblical themes about fatherhood. As we've walked through each of them, perhaps we've given ourselves an examination of conscience or passed judgment on our earthly fathers. While such a response might have some merit, we are also invited to review this summary and realize that all of these traits are powerful glimpses into the immense love and care that God the Father has for each of us.

Do we realize that God is our Father? Will we let him be a father to us?

Who Art in Heaven

Now that we have a broader comprehension of fatherhood, we can ask some questions about where he lives and where he wants us to live forever. The Bible uses the word *heaven* to describe the presence of God and our place with him. But what is heaven? How are we to understand such a mysterious place?

As a help to us in grasping the infinite beauty of heaven, we'll focus on the sovereignty of God and our eternal belonging with God.

God's Sovereignty

When we speak about God "who art in heaven," we are talking about his sovereignty, meaning his power and authority. We are naming his splendor, majesty, and glory. We are attempting to express the three-time exclamation of the angels: "Holy, holy, holy, is the Lord God Almighty, who was and is and is to come" (Rv 4:8). These are exclamations of marvelous proportions, and yet they still fail to express what is infinitely inexpressible, which is the utter and all-holiness of the living God. When we pause to really consider the cosmic and explosive nature of God's magnificence, we are inevitably forced to silence. We are called to praise and adore, to magnify and to acclaim, but we should be aware that God dwells in everlasting awe and regality.

In the story of salvation, a few holy ones were given a brief viewing of God's splendor. The apostle John was one of these holy ones. He gives us this description:

> At once I was in the Spirit, and behold, a throne stood in heaven, with one seated on the throne! And he who sat there appeared like jasper and carnelian, and round the throne was a rainbow that looked like an emerald. Round the throne were twenty-four thrones, and seated on the thrones were twenty-four elders, clothed in white garments, with golden crowns upon their heads. From the throne issue flashes of lightning, and voices and peals of thunder, and before the throne

burn seven torches of fire, which are the seven spirits
of God; and before the throne there is as it were a sea
of glass, like crystal. (Rv 4:2–6)

It's clear in the sacred text that the apostle-mystic is
scrambling for words to describe what he saw. He is drawing
on earthly jewels to express the beauty, festivity, and solemnity
of the experience. And yet his words cannot capture the awesome reality of God's heaven, where he dwells for eternity!

Similar to the struggle of St. John the Apostle, we also do
not have the proper words to describe heaven. In our shortcomings, we refer to heaven as a "place" or "dwelling," but we
know that God's heaven is beyond such designations. Heaven
is far above any "place." It is more properly spoken of as *a way
of being* rather than as a place or dwelling. And yet this reality
is very difficult for our minds to grasp, since we are not God
and cannot adequately give voice to his divine reality.

In our efforts to understand heaven, therefore, we use
terms such as place, abode, or dwelling. Additionally, the Bible
offers us some assistance by providing us with a particular
language and certain expressions for heaven. Among these
expressions, we find, among others: life, light, peace, wed-
ding feast, wine of the kingdom, the Father's house, heavenly
Jerusalem, and paradise (CCC 1027). While these can give us
guidance, they are also only symbols and figurative represen-
tations. In this way, we are bumping up against the popular
theological expression, "Whatever can be said of God, God is
infinitely more."

And so, in addressing our Father in heaven, we should
have a sense of the absolute and sheer immensity of his glory.
We should realize that we stand in the presence of the All-
Holy One, the Most High, the Sovereign of All Creation, the

Tower of Strength, the Ancient of Days, and the Messenger of the Covenant (cf. Dt 32:8; Is 9:6; Dn 7:9; Ps 61:3; Mal 3:1). To put it simply, we are in the presence of the awesome God, Lord of All, who has created us, cares for us, seeks to redeem us, and wants to have fellowship with us and see us face-to-face forever in heaven (cf. 1 Jn 3:2; 1 Cor 13:12; Rv 22:4). This summary of God's sovereignty is a brief portion of the biblical teaching on God's majesty. Even so, its words fail to express the reality. In his prayer, the Lord Jesus names this glory and reminds us of our Father, "who art in heaven." In realizing God's splendor, therefore, we can now more fully appreciate the preciousness of God's invitation to be with him forever. This awareness leads us to the second part of our review of heaven.

Eternal Belonging

When we address our Father in heaven, the pronoun *our* indicates that we have a place in God's family and, therefore, we have a place in his home. This means our whole life has been arranged and designed in such a way as to help us prepare well for heaven. It means that whatever happens to us in this world as we seek to love God, we have an eternal homeland waiting for us in heaven (cf. Rom 8:28).

Heaven, therefore, will be a place of reconciliation and homecoming. If traveled according to his law of love, then after our life's journey, God will welcome us home (cf. Jn 14:23). As such, in heaven, we'll share in his glory and partake in his divine nature. We will participate in the joy of God's Trinitarian life (cf. 2 Pt 1:4). St. John the Apostle describes this union between God and those in heaven: "Behold, the dwelling of God is with men. He will dwell with them, and they shall be his people, and God himself will be with them" (Rv 21:3).

As such, heaven will fulfill our deepest longings and consummate all our desires for happiness. All our wounds will be healed and our scars redeemed. We will be truly ourselves, and finally be freed from our sins and the brokenness of this world. St. John the Apostle continues and teaches us, "He will wipe every tear from their eyes, and death shall be no more, neither shall there be mourning nor crying nor pain any more, for the former things have passed away" (Rv 21:4).

As we are fulfilled in heaven by sharing in the communion of life and love within the Holy Trinity, we will also see others who have been perfected by God's grace. This means that we will also participate in God's union with Mary, the angels, our canonized saints, and all the holy ones in heaven. This further means that we will be reunited with all our loved ones who are in heaven! We will see and dwell forever with beloved spouses, missed parents or children, esteemed family members, and close friends who have been mourned and missed in this life. We will see them again, rejoice with them, and praise God with them into eternity.

This is the reality and beauty of our belonging to God in heaven.

God our Father calls us to be with him in eternity. He invites us to prepare well in this life. As we pray in the words that the Lord Jesus—our Older Brother and the Firstborn of All Creation—taught us, we must realize the depth of what it means to declare that our Father dwells in heaven. This assertion is not only a declaration of his majesty but also a declaration of our call to be with him in paradise forever.

Hope and Boldness

As we step back and look up, we realize that we are the children of God. We see clearly that our Father dwells in heaven and that we are called to be with him. This awareness compels us to give new direction to our lives. Our new identity as the children of God and our new destiny for heaven pose a challenge to our hearts. We have to change. We need to reorient ourselves. As our new identity and destiny cry out for fulfillment, we find a spiritual groaning and drive within our souls: We want God to be the true Father of our lives. We want to be open and teachable sons and daughters. We hope in the reality of heaven. We allow grace to work in us and transform us. We conduct ourselves in ways that could lead us into the joys of heaven (cf. 2 Cor 5:2; Phil 3:20; Heb 13:14).

The acceptance of God as our Father, and heaven as our home, fills us with great hope and joy. They show us the frailty of evil and darkness and give us a filial boldness, which is the fortitude of children who know they are loved and protected, to live holy lives and to fight for goodness no matter the cost. When our Father is in our heart, and heaven is in our sight, all things are possible (cf. Mt 19:26). We are willing to take risks, to be daring, and to labor for the kingdom of our Father. In imitation of the Lord Jesus, we are willing to give a constant yes to all that he asks of us (cf. 2 Cor 1:20) and to surrender all that we are to his glory.

Will we give this yes to God? Will we live in the awareness of God as our Father and heaven as our home? Will we boldly live the meaning of the salutation contained in the Lord's Prayer?

The Seven Tenets

Having explored the powerful salutation, "Our Father, who art in heaven," we will now walk through the seven tenets of the Lord's Prayer that follow after the salutation.

Each of the following seven chapters will be devoted to one of the tenets. As indicated in our introduction, each chapter will contain a *School of Discipleship* that will show us the interconnectedness of the Lord's Prayer with other essential aspects of our spiritual tradition.

We now move to the first tenet: "Hallowed be thy name."

CHAPTER 2

The Holy Name

Hallowed be thy name.

MATTHEW 6:9

Thy Name

The salutation "Our Father, who art in heaven" is followed by a series of three declarations of adoration and praise. These consist of an exultation of God's name, his kingdom, and his will. This chapter will focus on the first tenet, the glorification of God's holy name.

"Oh, My Larry!"

Some time ago, I heard a warm and amusing story. There were two very close friends. They shared everything in common, enjoyed mutual laughter, and trusted one another without question. They held similar beliefs on almost everything. There was, however, one major difference between them. One was a Christian, while the other couldn't care less about God and religion.

The Christian friend attempted on various occasions to give witness to her friend and describe the difference God made in her life. She would disclose vulnerable stories of mercy and kindness and explain various consolations and encouragements she received in prayer. But, try as she might, her efforts were fruitless. Her friend was disinterested at best and slightly condescending at worst. In the course of time, the two silently agreed to disagree on the matter of God and instead focused on shared sufferings relating to family, finances, and health.

The declared neutrality, however, was violated every once in a while when the unbelieving friend would spout off at the mouth and disrespectfully, even sacrilegiously, use the holy name of God. The profane use of the sacred name was wrapped in damnations and additional curse words. Every time this happened, the Christian friend would cringe, close her eyes, and try to whisper a prayer. She brought up the divine offense and her severe discomfort in conversation, but every time her friend simply dismissed it.

Eventually, the Christian knew something had to be done. As close friends, she knew her friend's extended family and friends. So on one occasion, when her friend started to flippantly use the holy name, the Christian preempted her and said, "I know, right? My Larry, what the hades is going on?" Her friend looked at her, confused. What was she saying? It must have been a slip of the tongue. Then later, again the unbeliever was going to offend the holy name, and the Christian interrupted, "Yeah, my Larry, they need to get their stuff straight!" Again the unbeliever looked at her. This time she was more confused and uncertain about what her friend was saying. Some days later, on a third occasion, the unbeliever was going to let some blasphemy fly while driving, but the Christian cut her off and said, "My Larry! What are you doing? It's called a blinker!"

By this time, the unbeliever was completely beside herself. After parking, she turned to her Christian friend and asked, "What have you been saying? What's the point of all this 'Larry' stuff?" Her friend just looked at her silently. The unbeliever went on, "I'm really surprised. You know 'Larry' is my father's name. Why would you keep using my father's name like that?"

The Christian patiently looked at her friend and simply replied, "Exactly. Why would I do that to your father's name? And if I answer your question, could you also please tell me why you do it to *my* Father's name?"

Yes, the believer made a strong point. We can call it a legitimate, "Oh, Larry" moment! And, while entertaining, it presents the holy name in its proper perspective. The holy name of our loving Father is a part of him and a part of us. As such, it is to be adored, cherished, and revered. It is not a word of profanity but is truly the holy name of the God of all humanity. As his children, we are called to protect and honor his name.

In our lives, do we realize the holiness of God's name? Do we understand the power we have as his children to address him by name and to speak to him?

All in a Name

Presumably, if you want to get to know someone, the first thing you're going to do is exchange names. It's only natural to reveal that important piece of information if you want to establish a relationship. And so it is with our relationship with God. It is vital that he tell us his name. This is where we must begin.

Except with God, we were not merely given his name in an instant. Instead, in the story of salvation, God revealed himself progressively to his people. He disclosed himself to the human family in stages of revelation, giving portions of his own self-knowledge to us over time. This progressive disclosure, which is a kind of familial sharing, can be seen in the unveiling of his name.

On his journey home after years of exile, the patriarch Jacob grows tired and seeks rest. While alone and in the desert, someone approaches and begins to disturb his peace (cf. Gn 32:23–25). The stranger pushes and shoves him and the two wrestle throughout the night. As dawn breaks, Jacob asks the person for his name: "Tell me, I pray, your name" (cf. Gn 32:29). But the figure never reveals his name. Instead, as dawn breaks, the person blesses Jacob and gives the patriarch a new name. He would no longer be Jacob, which is Hebrew for "liar," but would now be called Israel, which can be translated in Hebrew as "God prevails." In this exchange, Jacob (or Israel) realizes that the person he was wrestling was in fact God. He was so moved by the experience that he named the place Peniel, which means "face of God" (Gn 32:30).

Perhaps the most interesting part of this story is that God never revealed his name to Jacob. The full revelation of God's name would come later in salvation history.

Generations later, Moses emerged as a new leader. He was raised in the house of the pharaoh and held political authority. But after taking the life of an Egyptian guard who was persecuting the Jewish people, he fled to Midian, where he settled and soon married. On account of his new life, Moses quickly learned the duties of a desert shepherd.

On one occasion, he was tending his father-in-law's flocks in the desert near Mount Horeb when God called out to him. We can imagine the uncertainty and confusion of the prince-turned-shepherd, as he may have wondered, "Who is this heavenly being calling out to me?" Despite any possible disorientation, on hearing his name spoken, Moses responded with amazing openness, "Here am I" (Ex 3:4).

A command and an explanation quickly followed: "Do not come near; put off your shoes from your feet, for the place on which you are standing is holy ground. I am the God of Abraham, the God of Isaac, and the God of Jacob" (Ex 3:5–6). Moses obeyed. He removed his sandals and then immediately hid his face, for he now understood that he was standing in the presence of the living God, the God of Israel, the God of his ancestors. With Moses attentive and immobile, since he had no sandals, God began to give testimony of his immense care for his people: "And now, behold, the cry of the sons of Israel has come to me, and I have seen the oppression with which the Egyptians oppress them. Come, I will send you to Pharaoh that you may bring forth my people, the sons of Israel, out of Egypt" (Ex 3:9–10).

In receiving this momentous commission, Moses questions his own worthiness and abilities to accomplish the task. The living God responds to Moses with great tenderness and assures him, "I will be with you" (Ex 3:12). Moses follows up with an obvious question. It's an echoed variation of Jacob's question from years earlier. Moses asks, "If I come to the sons of Israel and say to them, 'The God of your fathers has sent me to you,' and they ask me, 'What is his name?' what shall I say to them?" (v. 13).

Rather than avoiding the question or humbling his servant, as he did with Jacob, God gave us a new portion of his revelation. At the request of his servant Moses, God gave us his name: "I AM WHO I AM." Then he added, "Say this to sons the Israel, 'I AM has sent me to you.' . . . This is my name forever, and thus I am to be remembered throughout all generations" (Ex 3:14–15).

In reflecting on these two moments from salvation history, we should be struck by their differences. Jacob wrestled with God by himself, through the night, and in a desert. He had his hip dislocated on account of the match and walked with a limp for the rest of his life. In this struggle, he begged God for his name and God declined.

And yet, generations later, Moses is in hiding from Egyptian forces for murder. He's walking around the desert as if he has no cares in the world, and God calls to him. He takes off his sandals and asks for God's name, and God easily complies, as a kind of, "Oh, yeah, let me give that to you."

Why the difference in a response? Why was Jacob declined, while Moses quickly received the name?

One answer can be found in the progressive nature of God's revelation to us. Jacob and the human family at his time were not ready to receive the holy name. Other revelation had to be given and accepted first, and lived well, before the holy name could be bestowed. In giving us his name, and unveiling more knowledge of himself, God established and disclosed a new level of closeness with us. In this way, we can say in colloquial terms that God "upped the ante" in a major way. In light of this understanding, it shouldn't surprise us that God declares something else with his name.

The first time God explicitly reveals himself as Father is precisely in this moment of salvation history. Moses is told by God to go before Pharaoh and announce, "And you shall say to Pharaoh, 'Thus says the Lord, Israel is my first-born son, and I say to you, "Let my son go that he may serve me"'" (Ex 4:22–23). God is identifying his people as his "son" and declaring himself their Father. This shows us that as God chose to disclose his name, he also bonded it with his fatherhood. As such, we must understand that God's name and his fatherhood are intimately interconnected. As we call upon his name, we are invoking his fatherhood. And as we receive his fatherly care, we receive his name and are called to revere and protect it.

The Power of a Name

In salvation history, the holy Name "I AM" was shown extreme reverence. It was purposely spelled as YHWH, without vowels, so that it could not be pronounced. As such, the holy name—transliterated as "Yahweh"—was only spoken on the singular liturgical feast day of Yom Kippur, the Day of Atonement.

The Day of Atonement, also called the Sabbath of Sabbaths, was the highest and most solemn feast day in the Old Testament (cf. Lv 16). It was the day of purification for Israel and for the sanctuary. On this holy day, which was celebrated once a year in the fall, a goat was prepared and sin was confessed over his head (this is the basis of the popular term *scapegoat*). Once readied, the goat would be sacrificed and the high priest would pass through the veil and enter the Holy of Holies. Once inside the Holy of Holies, he would sprinkle the blood of the goat on the mercy seat. In addition—and only on this high feast day—would the high priest whisper the holy name of God. There was extreme caution shown on such an occasion when a mortal human being dared to speak the holy name. As such, the Israelites would tie a rope around the high priest's ankle before he entered the Holy of Holies so that if God should strike him dead for uttering his all-holy name, they could drag him out of the holy place.

These ritual actions on the Day of Atonement purified Israel of its sin (cf. Lv 16). This connection of God's name with blood for a work of purification should not be overlooked. God's name is powerful. It's glorious. And this Old Testament pattern will be followed and fulfilled by Jesus Christ later in salvation history.

Additionally, as a sign of deference to the holy name, common words were used instead to address or reference God. The two predominant Hebrew words in such practices were *elohim*, which simply means "God," and *adonai*, which means "my Lord." Incidentally, when Greek became the predominantly spoken language in Israel, *adonai* was translated into Greek and became *kyrios*, which is the basis of our English word *lord*.

These various ceremonies and customs reflect the degree of esteem and honor that was shown to God's holy name. It's the fitting worship and adoration of children for the name of their heavenly Father. It's the proper disposition of a people who have been accepted as God's family and of creatures who have been made his sons and daughters.

As we reflect on this portion of our sacred history, we can ask ourselves where we stand in reference to the sacredness, the hallowedness, of God's name. Do we realize what has been given to us? Do we show a profound esteem to the holy name, and do we defend it in our lives today?

Jesus as the "I AM"

Understanding the extreme reverence given to God's name in salvation history, we can better grasp the declaration of divinity made by Jesus Christ. In St. John's Gospel, the Lord Jesus is questioned about his authority, with some even claiming that he was a demon (cf. Jn 8:49—58). The Lord responded, "I have not a demon; but I honor my Father, and you dishonor me. Yet I do not seek my own glory; there is One who seeks it and he will be the judge. . . . If I glorify myself, my glory is nothing; it is my Father who glorifies me, of whom you say that he is your God. But you have not known him; I know him. . . . Your father Abraham rejoiced that he was to see my day; he saw it and was glad" (Jn 8:49–56).

The response of his challengers was abrupt: "You are not yet fifty years old, and you have seen Abraham?" (Jn 8:57). And here the Lord Jesus declares, "Truly, truly, I say to you, before Abraham was, I am" (v. 58). The original listeners understood very clearly what the Lord had declared. After hearing the sacred I AM being spoken, we're told, "So they took up stones to throw at him; but Jesus hid himself, and went out of the temple" (v. 59).

In this intense encounter, it's both tender and powerful that the Lord Jesus declares his divinity while teaching and praising God the Father. And once again in salvation history, we see God's fatherhood connected with his name. The Lord Jesus appeals to the fatherhood of God in the same moment that he is using the holy name and identifying himself with it. As such, he is announcing that he himself is God and true divine Son, equal with the Father in majesty and glory.

In this way, the Lord becomes the face of the living I
AM to each of us. As St. John called the Lord Jesus "the Word
made flesh" (Jn 1:14), so we could rightly call him "the holy
name made flesh." As such, the holy name of Jesus is given the
same adoration and honor as God's people have always given
to the great and eternal I AM.

In the Upper Room, as he prepared for his passion, the
Lord prayed to the Father on our behalf: "And now I am no
more in the world, but they are in the world, and I am coming to you. Holy Father, keep them in your name, which you
have given me, that they may be one, even as we are one" (Jn
17:11).

In this prayer offered by the Lord, we see a reflection of
the tenet "hallowed by thy name." As the eternal Son of God
and as our older brother, the Lord Jesus desires to show us the
glory of the holy name and to teach us how to honor it, to be
filled with gratitude by it, to call down power through it, and
to filially use it to address and speak with the All-Holy God,
who is our loving Father.

Living as We Pray

With each tenet of the Lord's Prayer, we have to try to apply
its truth and wisdom to our world today. We have to take
what the Lord Jesus taught us in his prayer and make it a regular way of life.

So, what is our "living as we pray" strategy for "hallowed
be thy name"?

In salvation history, we see the connection between God's
fatherhood and his name. The holy name is not an extra piece

of divine clothing that has no value, nor is it merely some manmade designation that we impose upon God. The living God—Creator and Lord of all things—has revealed his name to us. As his name, it is a reflection of him and of his glory and power.

God gave us his name as a sign of his love for us and as a means for us to draw closer to him. With his name, we can speak to him, give him thanks, repent of our sins, and make supplication to him. We are blessed to build a strong relationship with him, since he has come to us and given us a name by which we can know and address him. This blessed access is something we could not merit or demand. We are not worthy of it, and yet God gives it to us because of his sheer goodness and his tremendous love for us.

In our lives, therefore, we are called to pray in his name and to acknowledge its beauty and power. As his children, we are privileged to receive and speak his name. Throughout our lives, in different states of affairs and with different groups, we are to show constant esteem and deference to his name.

Some examples of people who have demonstrated this reverence for God's name include:

- The parent overwhelmed with work, bills, car troubles, and difficult children, who realizes that she cannot carry all these tasks alone and so turns to God and with great hope, beginning her prayer with, "Father."

- The teenager asked to "swear to God" in casual conversation and refuses because the pettiness of the situation is demeaning to the holy name.

- The business person who pulls his colleague aside and gently tells him that his profane use of the holy name is offensive to God and asks that he refrain from its future use.

- The young family who resolves to give a slight head bow of devotion every time the name of Jesus is spoken.

- The retired person who realizes that for decades he profanely used the holy name without care or reverence and so decides to take on a daily devotion of praise to the holy name in reparation for his habitual offenses.

In acknowledging the holiness of God's name, we come to a broader and deeper awareness of his glory and of our unmerited opportunity to approach him and enter into a relationship with him. When such an awareness is generously received, it leads us to greater resolution and a desire to constantly honor and adore God in all we say and do.

Examination of Conscience

- Do I regularly pray and use the power of God's name in my life?

- Do I study salvation history and sacred doctrine so as to better understand the sacredness of God's name?

- Do I show an appropriate level of devotion to God's name when it is spoken?

- Have I profanely or blasphemously used God's name in my speech?

- Do I speak up and defend God's name when others use it offensively?

- Do I follow the vows I've made in God's name, especially those pertaining to my vocation?

- Am I cautious about the oaths and promises I make in God's name?

- Have I purposely lied under oath?

- Have I insulted or shown disrespect to people or things consecrated to God?

- Am I cautious about how God's name is used in my entertainment, such as the songs I listen to or the movies I watch?

School of Discipleship

As we mentioned in the introduction, this section, found at the conclusion of each chapter, will outline a series of links between the tenets of the Lord's Prayer, the Beatitudes, the Christian virtues, and the Gifts of the Holy Spirit.

Through this chart and its corresponding explanations, you'll see how all these aspects of the spiritual life point back, in a variety of ways, to the tenets of the Lord's Prayer. These connections are no coincidence but rather a testament to the balance and harmony of Christ's teachings and way of life.

In this way, the chart will provide you with a summary of what the kingdom of God looks like and how we are called to live and manifest it in our world today.

With this in mind, let's look at the first tenet: **Hallowed by thy name.**

As we grow in a greater devotion to God's holy name, the Holy Spirit bestows on us the gift of **fear of the Lord,** sometimes called "awe" or "wonder." A person with wonder and awe knows that God is the perfection of all we desire. This gift guides us to see God's glory and his work in our lives. We can see how it goes hand and hand with a reverence for God's name since the holy name reminds us of our own sinfulness and lack of holiness.

Once we receive this gift, the virtue of **temperance** is perfected in our soul, which is properly using the created things of the world according to the purpose for which they have been given. It is knowing how to put "first things first"—namely, putting God first and putting our own wants and desires second. More common terms would be moderation or self-control. If we keep a deference for God's holy name and if we fear the Lord, we will refrain from wanting and asking for too much, because we will know we should only want whatever God send us, and no more.

This tenet of the Lord's Prayer, gift of the Holy Spirit, and virtue help us to better understand the beatitude "**Blessed are the poor in spirit, for theirs is the kingdom of heaven**." In seeking to live this beatitude, we will be compelled to acknowledge God's majesty and our own lowliness. It calls us to acknowledge our spiritual poverty. We have nothing we can offer to God. We are beggars before the goodness and kindness of the All-Holy God. This beatitude, therefore, perfectly mirrors the adoration of God's holy name since it reflects both God's sovereignty as well as the familial relationship he offers to the poor in spirit.

Lastly, the path that begins from this tenet of the Lord's Prayer and crosses through these other aspects of the spiritual matrix helps us overcome the capital sin of **pride.** It should be clear how an inflated sense of self keeps us from revering God's name, as well as fearing the Lord or being poor in spirit.

Pride is a rebellion against God in order to serve ourselves, and in doing so, we lack temperance because we have made the decision to put ourselves first. With pride, we fail to have dependency and trust and instead seek to take in as much glory as we can for ourselves. The dark spirit of pride creates a small world that revolves only around us, our talents, our perceived power, and the use of things and other people as a means for our own use and enjoyment. This is the sin of the fallen angels, of our first parents, and of every soul doomed to perdition. And for many, it can be a hell on earth.

As the promise given through this tenet of the Lord's Prayer and its parallel beatitude is the kingdom of heaven, so the punishment of pride is this small, suffocating world full of loneliness and emptiness.

In conclusion, the first row of our spiritual matrix looks like this:

TENET OF THE LORD'S PRAYER	GIFT OF THE HOLY SPIRIT	CORRESPONDING VIRTUE	BEATITUDE	CAPITAL SIN
Hallowed be thy name.	Fear of the Lord	Temperance	Blessed are the poor in spirit, for theirs is the kingdom of heaven.	Pride

Prayer

Heavenly Father,
You are the Almighty and Ever-Living "I AM,"
I praise, bless, and adore your holy name!
Help me to understand my dignity as your child,
And the privilege I have of knowing your holy name.
Help me to know you better and to draw closer to you.

Guide me to honor your name in all that I say and do.
Through Christ our Lord. Amen.

Three Helpful Truths to Adore God's Name:

+ God's fatherhood and his name are intimately connected.
+ God has given us his name because he desires a relationship with us.
+ Whenever we call upon his name, we are calling upon his power and glory.

The Psalmist's Prayer

"Not to us, O Lord, not to us, but to your name give glory, For the sake of your mercy and your faithfulness!"

Psalms 115:1

The Lord's Supplication

"And now I am no more in the world, but they are in the world, and I am coming to you. Holy Father, keep them in your name, which you have given me, that they may be one, even as we are one."

John 17:11

Act of Reparation for the Profanation of God's Name:

Blessed be God.
Blessed be his holy name.
Blessed be Jesus Christ, true God and true man.
Blessed be the name of Jesus.
Blessed be his Most Sacred Heart.

Blessed be his Most Precious Blood.

Blessed be Jesus in the Most Holy Sacrament of the Altar.

Blessed be the Holy Spirit, the Paraclete.

Blessed be the great Mother of God, Mary most Holy.

Blessed be her Holy and Immaculate Conception.

Blessed be her Glorious Assumption.

Blessed be the name of Mary, Virgin and Mother.

Blessed be St. Joseph, her most chaste spouse.

Blessed be God in his angels and in his saints. Amen.

Additional Reading:

As we saw with the revelation of his holy name, God has slowly revealed something about himself to humanity over time. If you'd like to know more about this progressive revelation, this book can help:

Jeffrey Kirby and Brian Kennelly, *Doors of Mercy: A Journey through Salvation History* (Charlotte, NC: Saint Benedict Press, 2017).

CHAPTER 3

THE KINGDOM

Thy kingdom come.

MATTHEW 6:10

Thy Kingdom

The first tenet of the Lord's Prayer, "hallowed be thy name," is followed by the second tenet: "Thy kingdom come." Our adoration of God's holy name leads us to the exaltation of his kingdom. This chapter will focus on this second tenet, the glorification of God's kingdom.

Mission Focused

As a child, I grew up in Cold War West Germany. My father was serving in the Army's air defense effort. As their motto went, "If it flies, it dies." Living in such an environment, everything was under a cover of prevention and protection. As such, I thought every neighborhood had a curfew, military police presence, emergency fencing, and bomb-sniffing dogs. I also thought that every school bus had armed guards and a fortified escort vehicle. These were simply parts of life, and as a child, we just rolled with them.

Such a way of life was focused on protecting our allies, defending the democratic way of life, and preserving American strength on the global scene. This was our country's mission, the mission of the air defense units, and my father's mission. As his dependents, it was also my mother's mission, my siblings' mission, and my mission. It was all a united front. While fulfilled and played out in different ways, the goal was the same. The mission was clear. The sacrifices, the caution, and the rules were all in service to the overall mission. It was precisely this united front on every level that allowed the free world to stand fast and to eventually dominate over anti-human, communist forces and ideology.

While there were numerous signs and symbols in the fight for the preservation of freedom, there was one that stood out for me. In all my activities, whether I was outside in the playground, going to the swimming pool, or walking onto our adjacent military base to watch a movie with older friends, I always—without exception—carried my tan-colored US Army Dependent Identification Card, what popular jargon simply called our "ID card." The simple, laminated card displaying my name and photo, as well as my father's name, indicated to any authority that I was a member of the American community and the military effort in West Germany. It attested to the fact that I had a proper place and privileges within this American foreign effort. It showed me to be a part of the mission.

On the rare occasions when someone didn't have their ID card during a check, there would be a series of immediate counter efforts to ensure safety. Sometimes the person would be quickly escorted away or additional security personnel would appear out of nowhere. If the person was in a vehicle, emergency spikes would go up, and machine guns would be raised and held in the person's direction. All of these measures were taken because the person, their identity, and their place in the mission would be suspect and uncertain. Is this person a friend or foe? What is their posture toward our community? Do they come with intentions of peace or harm? All of these questions arose because an essential means of identification was missing.

If we can understand this situation, we can approach the reality of God's kingdom with fresh eyes and from a different perspective.

Mission and Kingdom

God's kingdom is not an abstract or poetic idea. While it is not of this world (Jn 18:36), it is nonetheless tangibly manifested in this world (Mt 3:2). It is precisely this manifestation—this exposition of God's kingdom—that we, the children of God, constantly pine for and labor to bring about in our world today. In the midst of the fallenness, brokenness, and sinfulness of our world, we fight for righteousness and cry out as his children: "Thy kingdom come!" This simple utterance gives an extraordinary expression to all our hopes, our heartfelt desires, and our hard work to allow truth to triumph and goodness to prevail.

As St. John the Apostle recounts, "The Spirit and the Bride say, 'Come.' And let him who hears say, 'Come'" (Rv 22:17).

The last chapter showed us that God's fatherhood and his holy name are intimately connected, and now we will see that both are directed toward a singular kingdom which has a focused mission in this world. The mission of God's kingdom is to proclaim among all people the utter majesty and goodness of God, to announce Jesus Christ as Lord, and to dispense his grace and bring about the salvation of all.

On account of this mission, God's kingdom is "an eternal and universal kingdom, a kingdom of holiness and grace, a kingdom of justice, love and peace" (cf. Preface to the Mass of Christ the King).

As such, the kingdom of God revolts against lies, dispels darkness, vanquishes evil, reacts to harm with promises of healing, seeks tranquility between God and humanity, labors for reconciliation between all people, and dwells always in the hope of creation's redemption and of God's triumph in all things. This is the mission of the children of God, and with righteous indignation, we shout in the face of wickedness and depravity: "God's kingdom come!"

Our Spiritual Identification Card

In the effort to spread God's kingdom, our spiritual "identification card" is our baptism. All the baptized—each one of us—have a part to play in bringing about God's kingdom. In our baptism, the Lord Jesus ransomed us from the kingdom of sin and darkness. He washed away all our sins and claimed us for God the Father. As our sins were purified, God the Father consecrated us in his name by adopting us into his divine family.

In our adoption, we became sons and daughters of God by grace. As such, we became siblings of the Lord Jesus, the eternal Son of God by nature. In this way, we were incorporated into the Lord's own body, which is the Church. By being members of the Church, which is the powerhouse of grace on earth that coordinates and invigorates the work for God's kingdom, we ourselves become members of God's kingdom. And so, with our spiritual identification card in place, our rallying cry and our acclamation of hope will always be "Thy kingdom come!"

Our baptism, therefore, marks us as members, messengers, and missionaries of God's kingdom. It displays to the world that we are a part of the effort to bring truth, salvation, and peace to all people. It indicates who we are, who we belong to, where we stand, what our community is, what we're willing to fight for, and what kingdom we desire to triumph in our world.

As the children of God, we are called to value our baptismal identity and to constantly yearn for God's kingdom. We are called to die to ourselves and to always be active instruments of this work.

St. Paul gives a powerful expression to this "groaning" for the coming of God's kingdom. He writes, "We know that the whole creation has been groaning with labor together until now; and not only creation, but we ourselves, who have the first fruits of the Spirit, groan inwardly as we wait eagerly for adoption as sons, the redemption of our bodies. For in this hope we were saved" (Rom 8:22–24).

The Battle for Goodness and Grace

In the beginning, God created all things good. He crowned his creation with human beings whom he made in his own image and likeness (cf. Gn 1:27). Created in such a way, we were given the capacity to love, reason, and hope beyond ourselves. In this way, we're able to uniquely share in the very life of God. We are neither angels nor animals. We do not have perfect knowledge, nor are we bound to automatically obey our instincts. We are human beings. With our spiritual powers, we are able to order our thoughts and passions, reason in a balanced way, and deny ourselves and our base desires.

In the Garden of Eden, these powers were elevated by God's presence. There was a beautiful harmony within us, with neither tension nor dilemma. Our bodies shared in the spiritual identity and immortality of our souls. We would never experience sickness and we were never going to die. There was peace between ourselves, God, and our neighbors. There was a balance between ourselves and creation. Creation existed without chaos or natural disaster.

This harmony was all lost, however, in the fall of our first parents. When Adam and Eve chose themselves over God, when they sought to steal his glory for themselves, and when they foolishly attempted to force the divine nature into our human nature, existential disorder ensued. Untethered mayhem, confusion, and pandemonium became the rule of the day. Our nature became disordered and creation became manipulated and twisted in its designs.

In short, the Fall introduced sin, instability, darkness, and evil into an otherwise good, ordered, and beautiful creation. With this understanding—that creation is good, but fallen—we can realize that good and evil are not equal. Creation is good, and this status cannot change since its goodness comes from God. Rather than existing alongside goodness, sin and evil are a contagion. They eat away goodness and reality. As such, they are anti-human, a privation of who we are, and are an anti-reality. In more casual jargon, we could say that sin and evil are a cancer, a virus against the existential health of humanity and creation.

Some might ask: If God is all-good and all-powerful, why does he allow sin and evil to exist? Wouldn't his goodness compel him to remove them and his power give him the strength to do it?

Such questions are compelling. A broad and immediate answer to these questions is that God has vanquished the power of sin and evil. The Lord Jesus, answering the call of God the Father, came among us as one like ourselves. Taking on our human nature, the God-man entered into our fallen world and defeated sin from the inside out. In the midst of our brokenness and sinfulness, Christ announced the overthrow of the kingdom of darkness and announced a new kingdom, proclaiming, "The time is fulfilled, and the kingdom of God is at hand; repent, and believe in the gospel" (Mk 1:15).

When he deems the battle concluded, God will complete his work. He will use his goodness and power to vanquish evil and bring an end to the world as we know it. Without any doubt, the living God has won—and will conclusively win—the battle against evil and darkness.

But in the interim, God displays his goodness and power by announcing his kingdom and giving us the time, grace, and wherewithal to fight the contagion of sin. He allows us to labor for the triumph of his kingdom of truth, virtue, and holiness. As members of this new kingdom, we are called to cooperate with his grace, pick up his mantle, and boldly enter into the fight for truth, beauty, and goodness.

St. Peter taught about this interim period when he wrote:

But do not ignore this one fact, beloved, that with the

Lord one day is as a thousand years, and a thousand years as one day. The Lord is not slow about his promise as some count slowness, but is forbearing toward you, not wishing that you should perish, but that all should reach repentance. But the day of the Lord will come like a thief, and then the heavens will pass away with a loud noise, and the elements will be dissolved with fire, and the earth and the works that are upon it will be burned up.

Since all these things are thus to be dissolved, what sort of persons ought you to be in lives of holiness and godliness, waiting for hastening the coming of the day of God. (2 Pt 3:8–12)

The living God, therefore, is not a clockmaker. He did not merely create the designs of the world, watch it fall, and then remove himself to watch the show as an idle bystander. Nor is he a puppet master. God did not respond to the Fall by seizing our free will and using us as mere pawns in his plan. Rejecting both of these postures, the true God has entered into our fallen world. He toils, labors, and combats with evil so as to bring about his kingdom of light, salvation, and true peace. As such, the Sacred Scriptures hail him as the "Mighty Warrior" (Is 42:13) and the "Wonderful Counselor" (Is 9:6) since he is in the thick of the battle and will not succumb to evil nor ever surrender to darkness.

God has adopted us in baptism and made us sharers of his kingdom. He has commissioned us and called us to fight for him, on behalf of him, and alongside him. He has empowered us, ennobled us, and sent us to bring about his kingdom. In this way, each of us—as his beloved children—are ourselves a living answer to the question about where God's goodness and power can be seen in the midst of evil and darkness.

The Kingdom in Our Hands

At the beginning of the Lord's public ministry, after he was
baptized and spent forty days of preparation in the desert, he
entered the synagogue in his hometown of Nazareth. While
in the house of worship, he was handed a scroll. The Lord
took the scroll and proclaimed:

> The Spirit of the Lord is upon me,
> because he has anointed me to preach good news
> to the poor.
> He has sent me to proclaim release to the captives
> and recovering of sight to the blind,
> to set at liberty those who are oppressed,
> to proclaim the acceptable year of the Lord. (Lk
> 4:18–19)

This passage was taken from the prophet Isaiah (cf. 61:1–
2, 58:6) and is considered a messianic text. This means that
the people of Israel recognized this prophecy as something
that would be fulfilled by the Anointed One (the "Messiah"
in Hebrew, or "the Christ" in Greek). The Anointed One, the
Lord and Savior of God's people, would come and give the
poor good news, free prisoners, cure the blind, liberate the
downtrodden, and announce great favor. These were seen as
tangible signs, "proofs," that the Anointed One had come into
the world.

This passage from Isaiah, therefore, was a highly charged
piece of Scripture. And Jesus knew it. He intentionally chose
this passage to inaugurate his public ministry. After reading it,

he returned the scroll and announced: "Today this scripture has been fulfilled in your hearing" (Lk 4:21).

It was not well received. His former friends and neighbors drove him out of the town and he moved to the coastal town of Capernaum.

The place that St. Luke gives to the proclamation of this messianic text is also significant. For Luke, this reading of Isaiah contains the first spoken words of the adult Jesus. He purposely recounts the use of these powerful words by Jesus at the very beginning of his public ministry. None of the other Gospel writers provide this level of detail about the visit to the synagogue in Nazareth. Instead of telling us about the Isaiah text, Matthew and Mark simply recounted that the Lord was announcing that the kingdom of heaven was at hand.

In comparing these two narratives, we can see that the Isaiah text is understood as the equivalent to Matthew and Mark's narrative of the Lord's kingdom announcement. Luke juxtaposes Isaiah to Matthew and Mark's proclamation of the kingdom. In this way, the parallel use of Isaiah and of the kingdom show us that the two are to be seen as mirrors of one another. This understanding can help us to see that "the kingdom" was viewed as the fulfillment of Isaiah's prophecy. The kingdom would be marked by the poor receiving good news, prisoners being freed, the blind being cured, the down-trodden being liberated, and great favor being announced to all. This is the kingdom of God. It's visible, tangible, truly present. And it actively counters the darkness and heals the wounds caused by sin.

Later in his ministry, Jesus emphasizes this exact point when some of the disciples of St. John the Baptist come to see him. They ask Jesus, "Are you he who is to come, or shall we look for another?" They continued, "John the Baptist has sent us to you, saying, 'Are you he who is to come, or shall we look for another?'" (Lk 7:19–20).

St. Luke tells us at that very time, Jesus cured many who had diseases, sicknesses, and evil spirits and gave sight to many who were blind.

In reply, therefore, the Lord said to the messengers, "Go and tell John what you have seen and heard: the blind receive their sight, the lame walk, lepers are cleansed, and the deaf hear, the dead are raised up, the poor have good news preached to them. And blessed is he who takes no offense at me" (Lk 7:21–23). In light of Isaiah's prophecy, we can see that he is making it very clear he is the Anointed One and that his kingdom is now at hand. The works described are his credentials. They are the marks of his kingdom.

In the same way, the Lord Jesus says to us: This is who I am. These are the works of my kingdom. Do these works. When they're done, my kingdom is at hand. When my kingdom is at hand, darkness and evil have no power and the sufferings of this world are healed and made whole. Bring my kingdom in your world . . . now!

The Lord stresses this point at the end of his earthly life, when in the Upper Room with his apostles, he said to them (and to us), "As my Father appointed a kingdom for me, so do I appoint for you that you may eat and drink at my table in my kingdom, and sit on thrones judging the twelve tribes of Israel" (Lk 22:29–30).

The kingdom has been entrusted to us. These works have been committed to our care. The kingdom of God that was promised through the patriarchs and prophets of old and that was prepared for in the kingdom of David is now fulfilled and placed in our hands. (Think about that for a moment!) As the adopted children of God, we have been given a name and a kingdom by our heavenly Father. We are called to zealously labor for the manifestation of this kingdom in our world. We are summoned to muster up all our hope and to constantly cry out, "Thy kingdom come!"

Do we realize that this kingdom has been conferred upon us? Do we understand the works of the kingdom that have been entrusted to us? Do we selflessly work and yearn for the coming of God's kingdom in our world today?

Living as We Pray

In receiving the call to spread God's kingdom, we realize that another kingdom is competing with it. Not only is there a kingdom of sin and darkness, but there is also the kingdom of our own fallen hearts. Oftentimes, we can assess tasks based on what we receive, or how they will help us, or what we will look like in the eyes of others. All of these perspectives reveal our selfishness.

In our efforts to build God's kingdom, therefore, we have to repent of our self-absorption, refocus our attention on the things of God and our neighbor, and recommit ourselves to the works of his kingdom. To put it simply, we have to realize we work for God's kingdom and not our own.

In the early Church, before the followers of Jesus were called "Christians," we were simply known as members of "the way." This designation aptly fits the identity and role of the Christian. As disciples of the Lord, we seek God's kingdom above all things and we follow the Lord's way of life, his way of love, in all that we do. As Christians, we continue the work of the Lord in our world until he comes in glory. We serve the poor because he served the poor. We care for the sick because he cared for the sick. We proclaim good news because he proclaimed good news. In all things, we do what the Lord has done. He spread the kingdom, and so we are called to spread the kingdom!

In acknowledging our mission and responsibility to spread the kingdom of God, it might be helpful to look at a few general situations where this call is being fulfilled:

- The young family who feels overwhelmed by the responsibilities of their lives, from work, school, and youth sports, to finances, health, and extended family; nevertheless, they decide to periodically stop everything and serve the poor by helping in their community's soup kitchen.

- The widow who doesn't know what to do without her beloved husband. Rather than falling into self-pity or bitterness, she focuses on forming opportunities for fellowship with other people who are grieving and seeks to serve other people in the community who feel lost or alone.

- The newly retired couple, whose friends are all enjoying extravagant vacations, extended golf days, and fine dining, make the intentional decision to live simple lives, give generously to local charities, and visit inmates in the county correctional institution.

- The monk who spiritually feels the sufferings and sorrows of the human family and offers heavy prayers for the coming of God's kingdom.

These are some practical examples of how we can cooperate with God's grace and seek his kingdom above all else.

Examination of Conscience

- Do I regularly seek the help of God's grace by worthily receiving the sacraments, especially Holy Communion and confession?

- Do I pray daily and ask for God's kingdom to come into my heart?

- Do I seriously work on abandoning vice and nurturing virtue in my life?

- Have I succumbed to despair or desolation in the face of evil or tragedy?

- Do I look for opportunities to increase hope in my life or in those around me?

- Have I ever given myself a "pass" to be unkind or impatient with a person or in a situation?

- Do I tithe and give generously to my parish and the poor in my community?

- Have I participated in the social outreach of my parish?

- Do I look for opportunities to spread God's kingdom in my workplace and neighborhood?

- Do I allow myself to be inconvenienced by others?

School of Discipleship

Continuing in our School of Discipleship, it is now time to look at the second tenet of the Lord's Prayer: **Thy kingdom come.**

If we pray for the coming of God's kingdom, the Holy Spirit will bestow on us the gift of **piety**. This gift of the Holy Spirit guides us in reverence toward God and his providential care. It might best be described as affection for God, which is instilled in us from our conception but can be nurtured throughout life. If we have this affection for God, we will inherit the earth, for he will return that affection and make us his sons and daughters. And as his children, we share in the inheritance of what is his, which includes the earth. Through piety, we remain a part of his kingdom on earth, the Church.

Once we receive this gift, the virtue of **justice** is perfected in our soul, which gives to others their proper due. As we honor God in piety, we are led to respect our neighbor through justice. The *Catechism* says that justice "is the moral virtue that consists in the constant and firm will to give their due to God and neighbor. . . . The just man, often mentioned in Sacred Scriptures, is distinguished by the habitual right thinking and the uprightness of his conduct toward his neighbor" (CCC 1807). Since the meek have an accurate view of their place before God and in relation to their neighbor, it is easy to see how justice would be perfected through a reverence for God's kingdom.

This tenet of the Lord's Prayer, gift of the Holy Spirit, and virtue help us to understand the beatitude **"Blessed are the meek, for they shall inherit the earth"** since those who labor for God's kingdom will share in God's sovereignty over the earth and his victory over sin and darkness. The person who humbles himself and surrenders to God's kingdom is truly a person of great meekness.

Lastly, the path that begins from this tenet of the Lord's Prayer and crosses through these other aspects of the spiritual life helps us to overcome the capital sin of **wrath**, or anger. This sin is the opposite of a submission to God's kingdom, meekness, piety, and justice. The person stuck in wrath is less worried about God's kingdom and more worried about his own.

Wrath is the use of force—emotional, physical, or by some other means—to assume power and to control life. As opposed to God's kingdom, wrath shrinks the world into the very small sphere of our own dominance and manipulation.

Meek people, and those who seek God's kingdom, order their emotions toward virtue, seeking both knowledge of themselves and justice for their neighbors. They understand that wrath must be tempered by reason so that it becomes righteous anger. They have a spiritual openness that allows God to give the whole earth to them as a home and place of peace. People consumed with wrath, however, are slaves to their passions and inclinations.

Wrath robs the person of their rationality and of their personality. It takes over all other emotions and becomes a tyrant within the person's very soul. The world becomes small, stifling, and dizzy. As God's kingdom gives us peace to fulfill the duties of our state in life, wrath's unchecked energy carries us past what we are called to do so that we infringe upon others' dignity, as well as our own, thus forfeiting justice.

As God's kingdom promises us eternity, so the punishment of wrath is a small world stuck in a battle, unsettled by angry passions, and marred by constant attempts to usurp control from God and our neighbors.

In conclusion, the second row of our spiritual matrix looks like this:

TENET OF THE LORD'S PRAYER	GIFT OF THE HOLY SPIRIT	CORRESPONDING VIRTUE	BEATITUDE	CAPITAL SIN
Thy kingdom come.	Piety	Justice	Blessed are the meek, for they shall inherit the earth.	Wrath

Prayer

Heavenly Father,
You sent your Son, Jesus Christ, to us as our Lord and Savior.
He established your kingdom on earth,
and conferred it on us when he ascended to your right hand.
Help us to cooperate with his grace,
Nurture piety and hope in our souls,
and to labor without fail for the triumph of goodness in our world.
Give us your peace and sustain us in your work.
Through Christ our Lord. Amen.

Three Helpful Truths to Seek God's Kingdom:

+ Jesus Christ inaugurated a kingdom of truth, goodness, salvation, and peace.
+ The Lord entrusted this kingdom to us, and has given us his grace to continue its work in our world today.
+ We dwell in joyful hope every day for the manifestation of God's kingdom.

The Lord's Promise

"But seek first his kingdom and his righteousness, and all these things shall be yours as well."

Matthew 6:33

The Apostle John's Greeting

"To him who loves us and has freed us from our sins by his blood and made us a kingdom, priests to his God and Father, to him be glory and dominion for ever and ever. Amen."

Revelation 1:5–6

Works of Mercy – Works of the Kingdom

Corporal Works:	*Spiritual Works:*
Feed the hungry	Teach the uneducated
Give drink to the thirsty	Pray for the living and the dead
Clothe the naked	Correct sinners
Shelter the homeless	Counsel those who doubt
Visit the imprisoned	Console the sorrowful
Comfort the sick	Bear wrongs patiently
Bury the dead	Forgive wrongs willingly

Additional Reading:

If you're interested in learning more about our call to spread God's kingdom, this book can help:

Jeffrey Kirby, *Kingdom of Happiness: Living the Beatitudes in Everyday Life* (Charlotte, NC: Saint Benedict Press, 2017).

CHAPTER 4

GOD'S WILL

Thy will be done, on earth as it is in heaven.

MATTHEW 6:10

Thy Will

The second tenet of the Lord's Prayer, "Thy kingdom come," is followed by the third tenet: "Thy will be done, on earth as it is in heaven." Our adoration of God's holy name and our fight for his kingdom compel us to surrender to his will. This chapter will focus on this third tenet, an abandonment to God's will.

Saying Yes

Probably the first time I thought of being a priest was in the fourth grade. After my mom picked me and my sister up from school, I wondered on the ride home what girl would be my girlfriend. Then out of the clear blue, I thought, "Well, I'll just become a priest and I can love them all."

I remember being surprised then—and I'm still surprised

now—that such a thought entered my mind at that age. I'm not even sure if I knew priests were unmarried, and I certainly didn't know what celibacy was all about. Looking back now, however, I can see that God was fashioning my heart for celibacy and priestly ministry, which are always a call to love selflessly and universally.

Of course, more fashioning, stretching, and discerning had to happen, and I wasn't a very compliant recipient of this work.

Later in life, I wanted to go to a university that would help me in both my Christian discipleship and prepare me for a good career. I attended Franciscan University of Steubenville and decided to study history and philosophy, with the hope of attending law school down the road. As my studies came to an end, everything was going right and the future looked very bright.

Yet internally I felt that things were going very wrong. Spiritually, I felt heavy and melancholic. I couldn't understand it.

Eventually, I reached out to a priest for counsel. This priest had known me for several years. He listened to me pour my heart out and then said, "There's one question you've never answered in your life, and until you answer this question, your life will always be ambiguous. Have you answered the answer? Will you say yes?"

Of course, I knew he was talking about the priesthood. Honestly, I was initially upset and thought, "I come to him for help and he gives me a vocations pitch!"

The priest wouldn't let me leave without making the promise that I would pray about it in front of the Blessed Sacrament. I made the promise, and as I was leaving his campus, I saw the church. I was in a hurry and thought that I would wait but something prompted me to go in. I pulled my car over and walked in. I knelt and prayed quickly. Nothing happened. I thought, "Promise fulfilled. I've got to go!"

But, again, something told me to go deeper. I calmed my soul, rested a little, and began to pray again. I went deeper and truly asked, "Lord, I've been telling you what I want from you. But now, please, tell me what you want from me." I didn't know where the prayer was coming from but continued, "I give everything to you. I give you law school, career, marriage and family, financial security. I give up."

Again, I had no idea where this prayer was coming from, but I know that it was right and that I was sounding more like myself than ever before. As I prayed, I started to cry in the deepest recesses of my heart. I clearly heard the quiet yet powerful call, "Come, follow me!" And, for the first time, I simply said yes. And I knew that this yes was an unconditional surrender.

Before this time of prayer, I had become lukewarm and I had my plan. I was a "practicing Catholic" but a terrible disciple of the Lord. In my mind, God was supposed to cooperate with and obey *me*. I had a good plan. I was a respectable person. God needs to comply and do what I tell him, or so I thought. My yes was a total change of heart. A deeper conversion to the ways of God. A total surrender to his will. My prayer had been, "Listen up, Lord, your servant is speaking." But now it was, "Speak, Lord, your servant is listening" (cf. 1 Sm 3:10).

Living with an obedience of faith, and truly discerning God's will, becomes simple when we call upon God's name and live within his kingdom. Following God's will, whether it's for our vocation, or showing mercy, or living with selfless charity, is nothing other than our Master turning to us and saying, "Follow me." And our response? The Lord asks for and relies upon a generous yes—not, "Let me get back to you!" or, "Could you ask someone else?" We just have to give a yes and trust in God's care.

Do we seek in the twists and turns of life to give God a generous and consistent yes? Do we realize the freedom and joy that come with an authentic surrender to him?

As It Is in Heaven

In the third tenet of the Lord's Prayer, we reference the will of God in heaven: "on earth as it is in heaven." We discussed heaven earlier in relation to the salutation of the Lord's Prayer, and so this reference shouldn't surprise us. The reference, however, does assume some things that we might want to review and understand.

First, heaven is the dwelling place of the all-holy God. It is an eternal existence in the presence of the all-powerful, all-knowing, all-wise, thrice-holy, infinitely perfect God. Any reference to heaven, therefore, is a reference to God himself and to his perfection.

Second, heaven is the place where God's angels live and serve. As such, heaven is an existence of absolute peace and sheer goodness. It is an ordered reality with eternal tranquility. All the angels know God's will, they perfectly do it, and they bask in the joy of loving and serving God in all his majesty and splendor. Any reference to heaven, therefore, is also a reference to the choirs of angels and their perfect obedience to the will of God.

This understanding of heaven can give us greater context as to why the Lord Jesus would appeal to heaven as a guide for our obedience and openness to God's will.

Rule in Hell

We know that at the beginning of creation, the angels were given a choice. As the plan of salvation was presented to them, Lucifer did not approve of the idea that one day human beings, below the angels in the order of nature, would surpass them in the order of grace. Lucifer rebelled, and he led others to rebel with him. The poets place in Lucifer's mouth the fallen declaration: "I would rather rule in hell, than serve in heaven." The Latin expression *non serviam,* "I will not serve," stands as a summary of the satanic decree.

Not content to exist in his own misery, Lucifer lied to our first parents and led them into their own rebellion. The devil knew that he was a creature and had lost in his battle against God, but he knew how beloved human beings were to God, and so he led a self-destruct campaign against the human race. In our Fall, the devil rejoiced. He celebrated the additional company in his misery but also the mockery of God's own image that was placed within our souls.

The sins of the earth followed the sins of the heavens.

The Firstborn of Creation

After Lucifer's rebellion, all the angels were given perfect knowledge. From that moment forward, the obedient angels would perfectly obey all the orders and ways of God. They would perfectly serve him and his creation. They were sent to reveal God to us, teach us about him, protect us, guide us, and lead us into the ways of holiness. As in heaven, so the angels ministered on earth. Through their ministry in the Temple and through the Law, they helped to prepare the way for our salvation in Jesus Christ.

Through the fall of our first parents, we learned the consequences of sin in our own way. We saw suffering and death, tragedy and deceit. We realized that we couldn't trust ourselves. We recognized a concupiscence within us—a battle between our intellects and wills—that inclines us to what we know is dark and evil. We became easier prey to temptation and are attracted to the habits of pride and vanity. The ways of earth, the path of the human race, followed the course of the fallen angels.

In this wayward course, therefore, our wills were placed in opposition to God's. We forgot the fundamental truth that God's will is the only true measure of creation. It is God's will that is the source and sustenance of existence. As St. Paul would remind us, "In him we live and move and have our being" (Acts 17:28). The will of God is the measure of our lives, the means by which we can become who we were created to be, and our only sure way to happiness.

The Lord Jesus came among us. He lived like us. He worked with human hands, cried with human tears and loved with a human heart. As God-made-man, the Lord Jesus redeemed creation and brought us back to the Father's love. He revealed the face of God to us and showed us how to surrender to the divine will. From the temptations in the desert to the struggles in the Garden of Gethsemane and on Calvary, Jesus was faithful to his Father's will. He was unrelenting. He would not allow himself to be distracted. In his public ministry, he even described his entire life in terms of the Father's will: "My food is to do the will of him who sent me, and to accomplish his work" (Jn 4:34). The Lord's nourishment is the Father's will. He seeks nothing else. He will follow nothing else, no matter the cost.

In this way, the Lord Jesus shows us the interior life of the Most Holy Trinity. The Son loves the Father as the Father loves the Son. He shows us the ways of heaven and the angels, as the angelic beings serve the Lord throughout his earthly life. In his teachings, life, and Paschal Mystery, the Lord shows himself to be the firstborn of all creation and the source of a new creation marked by an obedience to God's will (cf. 1 Cor 15:20–24; Col 1:15).

And so, as sin trickled down from the fallen angels, grace now floods down from the heavens—opened by Jesus Christ—and covers the entire face of the earth. St. Paul teaches us, "Where sin increased, grace abounded all the more" (cf. Rom 5:20).

Discernment, Properly Understood

On one occasion in the Lord's public ministry, he reacts to some of his supposed disciples' actions by asking them, "Why do you call me 'Lord, Lord,' and not do what I tell you?" (Lk 6:46).

It's a powerful question that can cause us to reflect on our life's choices. We know the way of life Christ calls us to, at least generally speaking, but how do we know God's Will in certain situations or decisions that confuse us? How can we assent to something unless we know it? Unless it's directly spelled out for us?

God doesn't always come right out and tell us what to do with our lives. But if we're honest about intending to do his will, he will guide us toward it.

The path in which we can come to know God's will is called discernment. But the way of discernment has to be properly understood since it has many caricatures. Discernment is not weighing our options, figuring out what's best for us, or accommodating moral truth and the divine will to our personal beliefs. Nor is discernment determining our own course of action with some courtesy to God. Discernment begins with a conversion to love God entirely and to make an intentional declaration to align our will with his. St. Paul explains this process: "I appeal to you therefore, brethren, by the mercies of God, to present your bodies as a living sacrifice, holy and acceptable to God, which is your spiritual worship. Do not be conformed to this world but be transformed by the renewal of your mind, that you may prove what is the will of God, what is good and acceptable and perfect" (Rom 12:1–2).

After this conversion and transformation, our minds and hearts are directed toward eternity. As the *Catechism of the Catholic Church* teaches, the sole criterion for discernment is the beatitude of God (CCC 1729). With this renewed focus, we can better understand discernment itself.

Discernment is seeking after God's will, whatever it might be, wherever it might lead us, and whatever it might cost us. Discernment uses doctrinal and moral teachings as its starting point and its principal guide. It seeks to apply these teachings faithfully to specific situations. It covers itself with the graces of the sacraments and prayer, the study of Sacred Scripture, the practice of virtue, and solid spiritual direction. The task of discernment is to identify which virtue is most needed, how it is to be expressed, and how it interacts with other virtues in seeking the beatitude of heaven. Discernment does not allow itself to get bogged down in details or to become narrow-minded in the things of this life. Discernment is edified by divine truth, liberated by the promise of heaven, and motivated by a genuine love for God and a zeal to always do his will.

Living as We Pray

As we seek to understand God's will, it might be helpful to remind ourselves that we are the beloved children of a heavenly Father who truly wants to reveal himself to us and show us his will. God is not a trickster. He does not maliciously hide from us or cause us meaningless confusion. He wants us to know his will and to be bold in accomplishing it.

With this in mind, we should regularly claim our status as his adopted children. As members of the baptized, we are called to denounce evil, its attraction, and its lies. We are also called to constantly confirm our faith in the living God: Father, Son, and Holy Spirit. With these two spiritual necessities, it would be a worthwhile practice to periodically renew our baptismal promises. These six promises walk us through the process of renunciation and affirmation. They can help us stay focused on God's will rather than our own.

In our discernment to know God's will, and in our openness to do it, we should regularly remind ourselves of our fallenness and brokenness. We should stay attentive toward our inclination to darkness and self-deception. If we're not careful, we can convince ourselves of anything. We even have the capacity to call evil good and good evil. This is a very dangerous power and one that needs to be kept in check. St. Paul reminds us, "Do you not know that all of us who have been baptized into Christ Jesus were baptized into his death? We were buried therefore with him by baptism into death, so that as Christ was raised from the dead by the glory of the Father, we too might walk in newness of life" (Rom 6:3–4).

And so, we are called to die to ourselves, to our wayward desires and misguided passions, and to seek to live in Jesus Christ and the glory of his resurrection. Truly, Jesus is our Lord, as well as our older brother. He seeks to share his son-ship with us and show us how to live as the children of God.

Understanding this call to follow the will of God, let's look at some practical situations in which people in the trenches have died to themselves and lived for God:

- A young woman at the top of her class, a cheerleader, and well-liked by all, who feels a call to consecrated service and accepts this vocation and selflessly offers up all her talents for the sake of the Gospel.

- A child hurt by a parent who, later in life, forgives the parent, letting go of his pain and dark memories, choosing instead to practice generous mercy.

- A parishioner who has been a "pew warmer" for most of his life, but now feels a strong summons to the sacraments and service and abandons his former luke-warmness and seeks a stronger relationship with the Lord.

- A young married couple suffering from tight finances who nonetheless practices Natural Family Planning, trusting in God for the path their family will take.

- A neighbor who does not like the personality of another neighbor and yet still invites them over for neighborhood gatherings and parties.

These are a few random examples of living this tenet of the Lord's Prayer. They are examples to us of how we are all called to live as we pray.

Examination of Conscience

- Do I regularly receive the sacraments, seeking God's grace to die to myself so as to live according to God's will?

- Am I attentive to the duties that come with the vocation that God has given me?

- Do I pray for an open heart to do whatever God asks of me? Do I teach those under my care this same type of prayer?

- Do I honor the Sabbath so as to receive spiritual and physical rest so that I can be ready and refreshed to do whatever God asks of me?

- Am I generous with my mercy?

- Am I generous with my time and attention?

- Do I regularly tithe—giving God my first fruits—so as to prevent money from ruling my heart?

- Do I cheerfully go the extra mile for others? If not, do I repent and ask for greater strength in future opportunities?

- Do I respect Church, civil, and local authority? Am I a good citizen?

- Do I look for ways to serve the forgotten, marginalized, and abandoned?

School of Discipleship

In our School of Discipleship, it's now time to look at the third tenet of the Lord's Prayer: **Thy will be done, on earth as it is in heaven.**

When we surrender to God's will in all that we do, the Holy Spirit bestows the gift of **knowledge** upon us. This does not necessarily refer to what we think most often of knowledge, as in that obtained through education and reason. Rather, this is the knowledge of recognizing good and evil for what they are. We are given the knowledge of how much virtue pleases God and how much sin offends him.

Once we receive this gift, the virtue of **hope** is perfected in our soul, for if we have the knowledge of good and evil, we can hope to live a virtuous life and find salvation in Christ Jesus. The *Catechism* says of hope, "It keeps man from discouragement; it sustains him during times of abandonment; it opens up his heart in expectation of eternal beatitude" (CCC 1818). With hope, we are able to persevere in a surrender to God's will, whether that is hoping for God's assistance and blessing during times of trial or hoping for his mercy after we have sinned. It is in our hope that we receive God's comfort. Hope fills us with certitude that goodness will triumph.

This tenet of the Lord's Prayer, gift, and virtue, help us to better understand the second beatitude: **Blessed are those who mourn, for they shall be comforted.** In this context, mourning is synonymous with sorrow over evil and sin. In recognizing our call to obey God's will, we rightly mourn when we have disobeyed him. Knowledge and hope give us eyes to see eternity and the goodness in our world today. The living out of this beatitude fills us with deeper comfort, since we know of God's kindness and patience towards us.

Lastly, the path that begins with a surrender to God's will and crosses over through these other aspects of the spiritual life helps us to overcome the capital sin of **envy**. This sin craves for itself what properly belongs to God, or what graciously belongs to one's neighbor. It deflates hope and builds a kingdom of misery in the soul of the one who is enslaved to it. Just as we are blessed if we accept God's will and grieve the loss of any good, the envious are unhappy in the good they see in someone else. If we live in God's will, we can share another's burdens and sadness, but if we are envious, we are happy over another's failures and sad at another's success.

If we don't grieve over evil and surrender ourselves to God, then we will abandon hope, rationalize or succumb to darkness, lose gratitude, and perpetually crave what we do not have.

As the promise of obedience to God's will is consolation, so the punishment of envy is a restless spirit always bitter about the good that others have. The envious have an awkward discomfort with both themselves and the world around them.

In conclusion, the third row of our spiritual matrix looks like this:

TENET OF THE LORD'S PRAYER	GIFT OF THE HOLY SPIRIT	CORRESPONDING VIRTUE	BEATITUDE	CAPITAL SIN
Thy will be done on earth as it is in heaven.	Knowledge	Hope	Blessed are those who mourn, for they shall be comforted.	Envy

Prayer

Heavenly Father,
You love us beyond all telling.
You desire us to live in the dignity of your children.
You teach us and show us the way to fulfillment and happiness.
Help us to know your will. Help us to generously do it.
Help us to have your heart as we seek to spread your kingdom.
Fill us with your Spirit. Your will be done.
Through Christ our Lord. Amen.

Three Truths to Help a Deeper Surrender to God's Will:
+ God's presence, and his divine will, are perpetual occasions of sheer goodness and tranquility.
+ God calls us to model our lives on earth after the perfect obedience in heaven.
+ God's will is our means to fulfillment and lasting happiness.

The Eternal "Yes" of Jesus:
"For all the promises of God find their Yes in him. That is why we utter the Amen through him, to the glory of God."

2 Corinthians 1:20

The Lord's Surrender
"And he withdrew from them about a stone's throw, and knelt down and prayed, saying, 'Father, if you are willing, remove this chalice from me; nevertheless not my will, but yours, be done.'"

Luke 22:41–42

Baptismal Promises

Do you renounce sin,
so as to live in the freedom of the children of God?
Do you renounce the lure of evil,
so that sin may have no mastery over you?
Do you renounce Satan,
the author and prince of sin?
Do you believe in God,
the Father Almighty,
Creator of heaven and earth?
Do you believe in Jesus Christ, his only Son, our Lord,
who was born of the Virgin Mary,
suffered death and was buried,
rose again from the dead
and is seated at the right hand of the Father?
Do you believe in the Holy Spirit,
the holy Catholic church,
the communion of saints,
the forgiveness of sins,
the resurrection of the body,
and life everlasting?

Additional Reading

If you're interested in knowing more about discipleship,
prayer, and discernment, this book can help:

Jeffrey Kirby, *Lord, Teach Us to Pray: A Guide to the Spiritual
Life and Christian Discipleship* (Saint Benedict Press, 2014).

CHAPTER 5

GIVE US

Give us this day our daily bread.

MATTHEW 6:11

Daily Bread

The third tenet of the Lord's Prayer, "Thy will be done, on earth as it is in heaven," concludes the first portion. Focusing on God's name, kingdom, and his holy will, the first portion adores and exults God.

The fourth tenet, "Give us this day our daily bread," is seen as an intermission. Not only because it mentions food, but because it indicates a shift from glorification to petition. We now look at placing needs before God as we ask him to "give us," "forgive us," "lead us," and "deliver us." Moving into this second portion of the Lord's Prayer, this chapter will now focus on the fourth tenet.

God Provides

Some years ago, I was at a parish where the parking area for the rectory was relatively isolated. One evening, I drove in

from a hospital visit. It had been a long day full of appoint-
ments and pastoral needs. I was tired and ready to get into the
rectory, take off my shoes, and have a few minutes of repose.
But as I pulled into the rectory, I was surprised to see two
gentlemen standing by the back door. This rarely happened
since the front entrance of the rectory was off a major road,
but back here it was secluded and hidden.

I pulled in, got out of my car, and yelled over to them,
"Gentlemen, what's going on?"

They both looked at me and apologized. They had gone
to the front door but no one answered.

"Okay, is there an emergency?"

They suddenly looked embarrassed, before responding,
"Pastor, we're really hungry. Do you have any leftover food
you can give us?"

The irony was that I really didn't have any leftover food. I
had recently cleaned out the rectory refrigerator and I didn't
have any prepared food. The two appeared genuine in saying
they were hungry. As a Christian, I knew I didn't have an
option. And so, I told my two guests, "Gentlemen, if you go
and rest at the picnic table around the building, I'll drive over
to one of the fast food places and bring you back some pizzas." The two lit up, smiled from ear to ear, and thanked me.
As they walked around the building, I drove off.

Honestly, I was very tired. I really didn't want to go get
any food. I wished that my guests had gone somewhere else,
and there was a selfish voice pressing in my mind, saying,
"I bet they just wanted money. You watch, I'll get back and
they'll be gone! And I'm not even in the mood for pizza!"

But I suppressed that voice and went and got the pizzas
and some soft drinks. When I returned, I was surprised to see

the two gentlemen sitting and talking. They saw me and were filled with joy. I parked, got the pizzas and drinks, and then walked over. The two stood up and were clapping and thanking me. One of them said, "Pastor, I didn't think you were really coming back. I thought you were just trying to get rid of us." The other, choking back emotions, said, "I knew you were coming back. I just knew it. I knew that God wouldn't let us starve!"

I ended up sitting down with the two of them, joining in conversation, sharing some laughs, and watching them have a meal. Truth be told, the food was nothing but cheap pizza and soft drinks, but the providential lesson of the experience was tangible and highly biblical.

In our own lives, do we realize that God will provide for us? Do we have the confidence that God will not let us starve? Do we realize that we are called to be instruments of God's goodness? Have we accepted the reality that God will answer the prayers of others for food and care by way of our hands and hearts?

In this fourth tenet, as we petition God for our daily bread, we simultaneously declare: God is our helper, our deliverer, and our companion. God will not let us starve. He will provide for us, and call us to provide for others. He will care for us today and give us our daily bread.

Manna and God's Care

Similar to the request of the two men, the ancient Israelites made a supplication to God, but Israel's story was a little more dramatic.

After God ransomed his people in their Exodus across the

waters of the Red Sea, the Israelites began to breathe the fresh air of freedom for the first time in centuries. After the initial joy and festivities of such a feat, however, the Israelites began to worry about their sustenance. No longer in Egypt, who was going to provide them with provisions? How were they going to eat in the desert?

Even though they had just been freed from captivity by magnificent display, they began to complain, even going so far as saying, "Would that we had died by the hand of the Lord in the land of Egypt ... for you have brought us out into this wilderness to kill this whole assembly with hunger" (Ex 16:3).

Perhaps it's difficult for us to understand this level of ingratitude. God has just saved them in ways that unquestionably affirm his power and providence, and yet they're worried about food. They mock his care of them as they engage in nostalgia over their full stomachs, full stomachs they possessed during a time of slavery!

How did God respond to such doubt and irreverence? Did he send down fire from the heavens? Did he turn a cold shoulder against his people? Did God allow his people to starve?

No, no, and no. The Lord is kind and merciful to his people, patient and overflowing in gentleness. He tells Moses, "Behold, I will rain bread from heaven for you; and the people shall go out and gather a day's portion every day" (Ex 16:4).

True to his word, we read, "And when the dew had gone up, there was on the face of the wilderness a fine, flake-like thing, fine as hoarfrost on the ground. When the sons of Israel saw it, they said to one another, 'What is it?' For they did not know what it was. And Moses said to them, 'It is the bread which the Lord has given you to eat'" (Ex 16:14–15).

In this account, we can clearly see God's delicate and attentive care for his people. We can also see how miraculous and creative his actions are toward us. No one could have expected bread from heaven! And yet, the ways and means of God's goodness are beyond our own powers of thought and imagination. As the prophet Isaiah reminds us later in salvation history: "'For my thoughts are not your thoughts, neither are your ways my ways,' says the LORD" (Is 55:8).

Throughout Israel's time in the desert, the manna continued to feed them. It gave them the necessary nutrition and strength to live and thrive. It was literally their daily bread.

As God creatively and unexpectedly provided for ancient Israel, so he desires to care, support, and provide for us. The living God wants us to turn to him and ask for today's daily bread. He wants us to trust him. In our interaction with him, we can express our sorrow, nostalgia, fear, and self-pity. We can even give voice to our ingratitude and anxiety. We are invited to speak openly about whatever is in our hearts because we are conversing with our heavenly Father who loves us. He knows our hearts and will convert them. He knows our fears and he will heal them. He knows our needs and he will provide for us. This is the witness given to us in salvation history. It's the summons inherent in the prayer given to us by the Lord Jesus.

Repetitively Redundant?

Many of us have prayed the Lord's Prayer since we were children. It's become a part of who we are and shaped the very way we pray. On account of its familiarity, we can sometimes miss some obvious points of the prayer. In particular, we may have missed the fact that in the fourth tenet of the prayer, it repeats itself. Yes, we pray give us "this day" our "daily" bread. Normally, we would only ask for our daily bread or for bread on this day. And yet in the Lord's Prayer, we say both. Why the repetition?

While the reason for the redundancy has been debated since the early Church, it is generally agreed upon by the great teachers of our faith that the petition is said twice as a reference to both earthly food and to spiritual food. In fact, the Greek word that's used for "daily"—*epiousios*—is a completely new word. It's not used anywhere else in ancient Greek. It's possible that the Gospel writers created the term as a translation of an Aramaic word originally used by the Lord Jesus, but scholarship is unable to give a concrete answer. The term is unique and most early theologians associated it with *supernatural* bread, and specifically equated it with the Breaking of the Bread, the biblical term for the Eucharist.

And so, it was believed by our ancestors that this tenet of the Lord's Prayer was not redundant at all but was actually a petition to God for both "this day's bread"—earthly bread— and for "supernatural bread"—Holy Communion.

It is for this reason that when the apostles zealously fulfilled the Lord's command to "do this in memory of me" and included the Eucharistic celebration in their fulfillment of the Great Commission throughout the world, the Lord's Prayer was (and has always been) a part of the Eucharistic celebration, prayed right before the reception of Holy Communion. The connection between the petitions of the Lord's Prayer and the graces of the Eucharist are clearly manifested, and the definition of *epiousios* as supernatural bread is given to the faithful.

The fourth tenet of the Lord's Prayer, therefore, is meant to nurture in us a profound trust in God's providence, as well as a deep hunger for the Lord in Holy Communion.

The Gift of Holy Communion

In Luke's Gospel, we read that Jesus, before beginning his passion in the Upper Room, reclined at the table with his apostles and said to them, "I have earnestly desired to eat this Passover with you before I suffer" (Lk 22:14–15). These words express the deep love he has for each of his apostles. And these same words, echoing through the ages, are said to us every time we participate in the Holy Mass. By being there with the Lord, he says to us, "I have looked very forward to this Passover with you."

These sentiments shouldn't surprise us. Throughout salvation history, God has always been searching for us. This search reached its fulfillment in the paschal mystery—that is, his passion, death, and resurrection. This paschal mystery is re-presented at every Holy Mass as the Lord works to save us from sin and darkness.

In the Mass, as the adopted children of God, we share in the Lord's own sacrifice. As members of his Body, we join with him as he offers everything to the Father, to *our* Father. We are invited to offer our own lives with the Lord. We lift up our prayers, works, joys, and sufferings. At the priest's invitation, we pray, "May the Lord accept the sacrifice . . . for the praise and glory of his name, for our good and the good of all his holy Church." This summarizes our action and the movements of our heart at every Mass.

But it doesn't stop there!

Flowing from our petition to receive *supernatural* bread, the sacrifice concludes with a memorial meal. This meal isn't just some family cookout or a casual sharing of food around some random table. No, this is an anointed meal, a meal of divine proportions, since the host and the banquet are God himself. He comes to us under the appearance of bread and wine and asks that we eat and drink. The Lord so desires a union with us that he comes to us as food. He enters into our lives, both physically and spiritually. This is an unimaginable gift. As the Lord taught us: "I am the bread of life. Your fathers ate the manna in the wilderness, and they died. This is the bread which comes down from heaven, that a man may eat of it and not die. I am the living bread which came down from heaven; if any one eats of this bread, he will live forever; and the bread which I shall give for the life of the world is my flesh" (Jn 6:48–51).

When asked, therefore, whether we have a "personal relationship" with Jesus Christ, we can truly answer, "Yes, I have an intimate and personal relationship with him. I've eaten his Body, broken for me, and drank his Blood, poured out for me!"

In Holy Communion—the receiving of the very Body and Blood of Jesus Christ—we are united with him. St. Paul explains such a union: "I have been crucified with Christ; it is no longer I who live, but Christ who lives in me; and the life I now live in the flesh I live by faith in the Son of God, who loved me and gave himself for me" (Gal 2:20). Yes, we are truly one with the Lord. He dwells in us and we live for him!

The invitation for us to sit at his table and share in his meal should not be underestimated. In the ancient world, only a person's family and very close friends would eat at his table. Extended guests or recipients of charity ate in a different

room or outside. Only the family and intimate friends ate at
the table (cf. Mt 15:21–28). And here we are invited to dine
at God's sacred table! This divine hospitality was so esteemed
that, after the Lord's glorious ascension, the apostolic preaching cited table fellowship with the Lord as a credential for its
authenticity. St. Peter preached, "We are witnesses to all that
he did both in the country of the Jews and in Jerusalem. They
put him to death by hanging him on a tree; but God raised
him on the third day and made him manifest; not to all the
people but to us who were chosen by God as witnesses, who
ate and drank with him after he rose from the dead" (Acts
10:39–41).

By having this extreme union with the Lord Jesus in
Holy Communion, we also have a share in the powerful and
beautiful communion of saints. This communion is universal,
across time and space, a connection of all believers. In the
communion of saints, we are bound to one another. We are as
close to St. Peter in apostolic times as to St. Cecilia in the second century AD, St. Benedict in the sixth century AD, and the
recent member of our family who died within the past year.
We are all the one Body of Jesus Christ, united in him (cf.
Rom 12:3–8). This is a consoling reality as we bid loved ones
farewell in this life. The sure knowledge of our communion
with them is a strong manifestation of the Lord's resurrection
and of the supernatural power of Holy Communion.

It is no accident that our beloved dead are remembered
in every Eucharistic Prayer during Mass, because they are still
with us. We are one Body, and nothing—not even death—
can separate us from one another in Jesus Christ (cf. Rom
8:38–39).

Strengthened by our union with the Lord Jesus and edified

by our communion with the holy ones through our reception of Holy Communion, we are compelled and spurred on
to greater holiness. We are driven to glorify his name, labor
for his kingdom, and generously obey his will. The graces
of receiving the Body and Blood of Jesus Christ wipe away
our venial sins, fortify our resolve against mortal sins, build
up our resistance to sensual passions, incite us to virtue, lead
us to prayer and selfless service, and give us a sensitivity to
the things of God and a displeasure towards sinful acts and
darkness. These are the internal transformations that happen
because of our reception of the supernatural bread that we ask
for in the Lord's Prayer.

Bringing "Daily Bread" to Others

In professing God's providential care for us and his desire
to give us bread each day—namely, to fulfill our needs each
day—some might ask: But aren't there children dying of hunger? Aren't there whole regions of our world that are inflicted
with poor health, corrupt governments, abysmal economies,
and suffering beyond imagination? Where is God's daily bread
to these people?

The response is found in the supernatural bread. As we
receive the Body of Christ, we are called to live as members
of the Body of Christ, and so we are commissioned to do the
work of the Body of Christ. Put simply, as adopted children
of God and as recipients of Holy Communion, we are called
to lay down our lives and to be daily bread to others. We are
blessed to be empowered and entrusted with being instruments of his divine providence in our world, especially to
the sick, suffering, and those in need. This summons means

that we must give food, provide drink, clothe, shelter, make visits, bury, instruct, counsel, admonish, bear wrongs, forgive, comfort, and pray. It means we must be generous, selflessly serve, advocate on behalf of others, inspire our neighbors to be benevolent, intercede, and offer up spiritual sacrifices for those who are suffering and in need.

The *Catechism of the Catholic Church* reminds us "*The Eucharist commits us to the poor.* To receive in truth the Body and Blood of Christ given up for us, we must recognize Christ in the poorest, his brethren" (CCC 1397).

And so, in receiving Holy Communion, do we realize the commission we receive to be the daily bread of others? Are we willing to apply the graces of this sacrament in service to the poor? Are we open to being the instruments of God's providence to those in need?

Living as We Pray

As the Lord's Prayer moves from the three tenets of praise to the four tenets of petition, it should strike us as peculiar that the four petitions are worded as *commands*: "give us," "forgive us," "lead us," and "deliver us." Is this how we are supposed to talk with our heavenly Father?

In short, yes! After all, this is how the Lord Jesus, our older brother, taught us to pray. But we should understand the spirit behind the wording. We do not command God as if he serves us. Nor do we command God as if he is indebted to us or must do what we say so that he feels more divine. No, God doesn't need us. He chooses to love us and welcome us into his family. As members of his family, as his true sons and daughters, we are to have a humble yet vibrant *filial boldness*.

This term is used by the *Catechism of the Catholic Church*, as we are reminded: "In his teaching, Jesus teaches his disciples to pray with a purified heart, with lively and persevering faith, with filial boldness" (CCC 2621).

Filial (familial) boldness means that, as his sons and daughters, we can speak openly and with trust. It means that we know how good he is and can have confidence in his goodness toward us. Filial boldness means that we don't have to play games or grovel. We acknowledge that we are completely dependent on him, and so we let our Father know what we think we need and we trust in him. This humility and docility are the difference between a person with an arrogant hubris in prayer and a child's open-hearted boldness in prayer (cf. Lk 18:9–14).

As his children, we ask our Father for our needs and petition him for the fulfillment of our daily necessities. We rely on him for our daily bread, for the needs of our lives. With trust, we pray and seek his loving kindness and providential care in our everyday lives. We also yearn and petition him for his companionship and intimacy in Holy Communion. We know the love he has for us and we ask him to come to us as supernatural bread. As recipients of his goodness in our lives and of his presence and power in Holy Communion, we rely on his fellowship as we seek to selflessly serve others.

Relying on God's grace, we are willing to push ourselves, leave our comfort zones, and become daily bread for others. We give a constant and unconditional yes to the privilege and responsibility of being an instrument of God's providence to those in need.

In our world today, there are many general examples of how others have lived out this tenet of the Lord's Prayer. Here are just a few:

- The young couple struggling with finances who, refusing to give in to despair or desolation, continues to offer heartfelt prayers to God for financial help.

- The teenager who refuses to give in to peer pressure and demand unnecessary expensive clothes from his parents so that the money can be used for other needs in the family.

- The retired person who realizes that throughout his entire life he has been indifferent to the graces of the Mass and so decides to go to daily Mass and encourage his friends to go with him.

- The person with serious medical problems and no consolation in sight who intentionally decides to trust in God and stay committed to prayer, asking him for healing of the illness or strength to offer it up.

- The neighbor who realizes that the young couple next door is hurting financially and decides to offer them financial help for some small repair projects around her home.

Examination of Conscience

- Do I participate in Mass on Sundays and Holy Days of Obligation? Do I ensure that those under my charge also participate in these Masses?

- If I'm able, do I try to participate in Mass during the week? Do I encourage my loved ones to do the same?

- Do I seek out opportunities to adore the Blessed Sacrament?

- Do I nurture a spirit of trust in my relationship with God?

- Do I indulge in self-pity, resentment, and bitterness, especially when I don't get what I want, when I want it?

- Do I regularly thank God for the gifts that he has given me? Do I offer these prayers of gratitude even when times are difficult?

- Do I offer up my physical, emotional, and spiritual sufferings? Do I realize that delayed answers to prayers are blessed opportunities for spiritual sacrifices?

- Do I allow a spirit of fear to rule my life?

- Have I sought out the poor in my community and actively tried to provide them with whatever help I can?

- Do I willingly seek to serve the sick, lonely, abandoned, hungry, homeless, and unemployed?

School of Discipleship

Continuing in our School of Discipleship, it is now time to look at the fourth tenet of the Lord's Prayer: **Give us this day our daily bread.** Twice in this petition—"this day" and "daily"—do we stress our complete dependency on God and our awareness that we are filled only in him. This fulfillment comes from the True Bread, the Eucharist. When we say we are hungering for holiness, we might as well say we are hungering for the Eucharist.

If we seek our daily bread from God's goodness, the Holy Spirit bestows us with the gift of **fortitude**, which the

Catechism tells us "ensures firmness in difficulties and con-
stancy in the moral life" (CCC 1808). Through fortitude, we
conquer temptations and fears, even fear of death, as so many
martyrs have shown. If this tenet of the Lord's Prayer promises
us that we will be satisfied, then it should not surprise us that
we will be given fortitude; just as a well-fed and satisfied body
will be strong when it faces threats, so will the well-fed soul
be when temptation attacks. The holiness we seek and then
consume is like valuable protein that strengthens us.

Once we receive this gift, the virtue of **courage** is perfected in our soul. Today, many use these two words (fortitude
and courage) interchangeably. The difference for our purposes
is that fortitude is a gift donated to us, which then enables
us to be courageous. Fortitude is the input, while courage is
the output, if you will. We are only able to be courageous in
the face of temptation and fear because we are enriched with
fortitude. As we stay the course with fortitude, we are led to
uphold virtue and honor our neighbor through courage.

This tenet of the Lord's Prayer, gift, and virtue help us to
better understand the beatitude **"Blessed are those who
hunger and thirst for righteousness, for they shall be
satisfied."** Just as the living God will answer our petition
for today's daily bread, so he will respond to any true desire
for holiness. He will not allow his holy ones to be hungry or
thirsty without granting them satisfaction and fulfillment. The
Lord provides, and for those who rely on him and cooperate
with his providence, holiness is bestowed and righteousness
is given.

Lastly, the path that begins with this tenet of the Lord's
Prayer and crosses through these other aspects of the spiritual
life helps us to unmask the deception of the capital sin of

sloth. This serious sin is a spiritual indifference and a willful laziness, especially toward our soul and our natural desire for God. Physical laziness is an aspect of sloth, but this is not a complete definition. A man could work eighty hours a week and be materially driven to achieve success and still be slothful because he is "lazy" when it comes to tending for his soul. This person stuck in sloth is focused more on his own self-sufficiency and comfort than on the kingdom of God.

The satisfaction of spiritual hunger and thirst cannot be given to us when we are unwilling to put our spirit to work.

If we neglect our spiritual hunger and suppress our thirst for holiness, then sloth wins and self-indulgence sets in. Try as we might, with all that we can muster, we will not be content with ourselves, other people, or our world. We will be stuck in a cycle of nervousness, denial, agitation, momentary euphoria, melancholy, and rampant anxiety. In short, we will be perpetually hungry and thirsty and unable to be fulfilled.

As the promise of seeking God's will is satisfaction, so the punishment of sloth is a jaded, tired, and empty soul that lacks the nourishment it needs to fight evils and temptations.

In conclusion, the third row of our spiritual matrix looks like this:

TENET OF THE LORD'S PRAYER	GIFT OF THE HOLY SPIRIT	CORRESPONDING VIRTUE	BEATITUDE	CAPITAL SIN
Give us this day our daily Bread.	Fortitude	Courage	Blessed are those who hunger and thirst for righteousness, for they shall be satisfied.	Sloth

Prayer

Good and Gracious God,
You are always there when we need you.
Help us to trust you.
In difficult or stressful times,
Confirm us in your care.
Hold us close when things seem scattered.
Strengthen us when our hearts our weak.
Console us when we are afraid.
You are our protector and guide,
We believe in you.
We hope in you.
Through Christ our Lord.
Amen.

Three Truths on Today's Daily Bread:

+ God desires to take care of us and we can trust him to provide our day's necessities.
+ The Lord Jesus shows us the depth of his love by coming to us as supernatural bread.
+ In our lives, we are called to be instruments of God's providence and daily bread to those around us.

The Lord's Instructions:

"And he said to his disciples, 'Therefore I tell you, do not be anxious about your life, what you shall eat, nor about your body, what you shall put on. For life is more than food, and the body more than clothing. Consider the ravens: they neither sow nor reap, they have neither storehouse nor barn, and yet God feeds them. Of how much more value are you than the birds! And which of you by being anxious can add a cubit to his span of life? If then you are not able to do as small a thing as that, why are you anxious about the rest?'"

Luke 12:22–26

The Lord's Eager Desire:

"And when the hour came, he sat at table, and the apostles with him. And he said to them, 'I have earnestly desired to eat this Passover with you before I suffer.' . . . And he took bread, and when he had given thanks he broke it and gave it to them, saying, 'This is my body which is given for you. Do this in remembrance of me.' And likewise the chalice after supper, saying, 'This chalice which is poured out for you is the new covenant in my blood.'"

Luke 22:14–15, 19

Act of Spiritual Communion:

My Jesus,
I believe that you
are present in the Most Holy Sacrament.
I love you above all things,
and I desire to receive you into my soul.
Since I cannot at this moment
receive you sacramentally,
come at least spiritually into my heart.
I embrace you as if you were already there,
and unite myself wholly to you.
Never permit me to be separated from you.
Amen.

Additional Reading:

If you'd like to know more about God's care for us, this book can help:

Jeffrey Kirby, *Be Not Troubled: A 6-Day Personal Retreat with Fr. Jean-Pierre De Caussade* (Ave Maria Press, 2019).

CHAPTER 6

Forgive Us

And forgive us our trespasses, As we forgive
those who trespass against us.

MATTHEW 6:12

Forgiveness

The fourth tenet of the Lord's Prayer, "give us this day our daily bread," is followed by the fifth tenet: "And forgive us our trespasses, As we forgive those who trespass against us." And so, we now petition God for his mercy and ask for his strength in forgiving others. This chapter will now focus on the fifth tenet of the Lord's Prayer.

"As We"

When I was a student at the Franciscan University of Steubenville, I was blessed with the powerful witness of strong and convicting homilists. True to their priestly vocation and their Franciscan spirituality, the friars regularly challenged us students to live our "upward calling" in Jesus Christ (cf. Phil

3:14). Some homilies made us uncomfortable, but they were the ones we talked about for days.

Among the many dynamic homilists at the university, Father Michael Scanlan was preeminent. As the president of the university, he saw himself as the spiritual father and shepherd of the student body and actively lived out this part of his ministry. Father Mike, as he was affectionately called by students and faculty alike, spent time in the cafeteria, attended sporting events, temperately displayed a few moves at student dances, and regularly hung out in the student union. Father Mike made himself visible and accessible. Although he sometimes looked tired, he always had a contagious laughter. And his piercing eyes made you pay attention to him because Father Mike always had some piece of wisdom or some profound thought to pass along.

Of course, nothing compared with Father Mike's time in the confessional, at the altar, or at the ambo. He was a priest first and foremost, and that identity modeled everything else he did and said. He was a gentle but challenging confessor. He was a priest who was attentive to the sacred liturgy and the beauty of our Catholic tradition. And, in an amazing way, Father Mike was a true herald of the Gospel and a preacher of truth. We knew when Father Mike preached, the chapel would be packed. He was always eloquent and engaging.

With this precedent understood, you can imagine the surprise and confusion when, on one occasion, Father Mike got up to the ambo and glanced around the church with a stern expression. You could feel the tension in the air. He looked down, paused, and then looked up again with those penetrating eyes. And then, looking out—as if looking at each person in the congregation in a personal way—he simply said,

"As we!" He paused, not breaking his stare. Then, after a few seconds (that felt like hours), he said again, "As we!" He then went and sat down.

"Wait! Was that it? Is he sick or tired?"

It was only later that many of us made the connection. The Gospel reading at that Mass was the Lord Jesus giving the apostles his prayer. And that pivotal part of the Lord's Prayer, that is both crux and crucible, is the prayerful declaration we make: "forgive us our trespasses, *as we* forgive those who trespass against us." We want to ignore the conditional part of that petition. We want to put it aside and neglect the weight of glory placed upon us by those convicting words, "as we."

Yes, those words should haunt us and cause us unease. We are asking God to bestow his mercy on us in the same way *as we* give (or don't give) mercy to others. In offering up this prayer, we are beseeching God—with our own words, mind you—to either bless us or to condemn us.

Father Mike had made his point. And yes, we talked about that two-word homily for years. It's been brought up at reunions since graduation and here in this book, almost twenty years later. The homily was that strong because this tenet of the Lord's Prayer is that strong and our call to give mercy is that strong.

Do we realize the self-imposed condition that we place on God's mercy in the Lord's Prayer? Do we understand how generous God is with his mercy? Do we seek to imitate that generosity in the mercy we give to others?

The Mercy of God

The reality of God's goodness was expressed in the Old Testament through the Hebrew word *hesed*. Although the word is usually defined as "loving kindness," the word is difficult to fully translate since it describes God's benevolence, tenderness, magnanimity, forbearance, and hospitality toward us. In the ancient world, the word left no question in anyone's mind that the living God of Israel, the great I AM, desired to be in communion with his people. The simple expression *hesed* was a declaration of familiarity and companionship. It meant (and means) that God wants to be with us, he loves us, and he welcomes us into his family. As such, it is a family-based invitation to enter into and be a part of a vibrant relationship with God.

This overture of the living God was in stark contrast to the myths of the ancient Greeks and Romans, who saw the gods as capricious, hurtful, self-absorbed deities that sought to inflict harm and suffering out of jealousy, pettiness, and boredom. In contrast to this, the God of Israel—who is the God of Jesus Christ—is one. He is good, true, beautiful, and he reveals himself to us as Father. And as a loving Father, he dispels the deception of fallen angels and pagan myths. He shows us constant *hesed*, loving kindness that endures.

It's important that we start with this broad, relational understanding of *hesed* because the word also has another definition. The word *hesed* is also translated as "mercy." Yes, everything that was just summarized about God's loving kindness is inherently included in the biblical definition of mercy, and that should rock our minds!

Oftentimes, in contemporary usage, when we think of

mercy, we minimize it and think of it only as the means of removing guilt. While that's certainly included in *hesed,* it doesn't explain why God would do it. The full definition of *hesed* gives a full and clear explanation of why God would forgive us. As the Lord Jesus leads us to the mercy of God and calls us to give this mercy to others, we should seek to understand the depth and breadth of God's merciful and loving kindness.

You might say that we think mercy has everything to do with the judge's courtroom, while God constantly reveals that his mercy is more about the Father's living room. In biblical revelation, mercy is one more expression of God's goodness toward us. It's all about his fatherhood. It's all about his family.

Justice and Mercy

When we begin to address mercy in terms of a familial relationship, it naturally begs a question about justice and discipline. Does mercy mean that there are no consequences for offenses?

The question is a good one and it helps keep our discussion within the context of family relationships. In a good family, people care for one another, love each other, and do kind things on behalf of one another. However, there are also times when people hurt or harm one another, and *these offenses are always seen in the context of the greater relationship.* For example, you might hear a woman say, "She really hurt me, but she's my sister." Again, the offense is seen in terms of the relationship. As such, mercy and justice work together.

Mercy is giving someone the freedom to convert and change their lives. It holds no permanent restraint or judgment against them. Mercy, therefore, is not telling someone that their offense is acceptable, nor is it giving an irresponsible pass to someone who has caused harm. Mercy requires justice, even as it fulfills its demands.

Justice is giving to someone else what is their due. This could mean giving someone compensation for work, or respect for their dignity as human persons. It could also mean appropriate punishment or discipline for an offense against virtue, our human dignity, or society's common good. Justice is not vengeance, therefore, since vengeance seeks to destroy another person by acts of commission or omission in reaction to a real or perceived offense. Vengeance disregards human reason, the other virtues, and the proportionate response of justice, as well as the care called for by human relationships. Vengeance obsessively seeks the annihilation of another person and, thus, is a far cry from justice.

When justice requires punishment or discipline, it is born from a loving kindness (*hesed*) for another. It seeks to restore the person to virtue, a right relationship with another, or a proper place within society. Understood in this light, we can see how justice and mercy are friends. In our spiritual tradition, St. Thomas Aquinas explained, "Mercy without justice is the mother of dissolution. Justice without mercy is cruelty." The two need each other and form a unified rapport in any true relationship.

In order for mercy to be substantial, therefore, it must fulfill the demands of justice. In order for justice not to fall into vengeance, it needs the guidance of mercy. The two are not opposed but work in a complementary fashion within human souls and society.

As such, we can legitimately forgive someone who has

caused damage to our car, while also expecting them to pay for the repairs. Mercy is a denunciation of vengeance and a desire to help another person to make just reparations for an offense they've committed and so guide them in reestablishing a healthy relationship with their neighbor.

God's interaction with his people throughout the Old Testament reaches its fulfillment in Jesus Christ. In this sacred narrative of ups and downs, of obedience and rebellion, we see the regular interplay between justice and mercy. God is molding us, forgiving us, disciplining us, and reconciling us with himself and one another through both justice and mercy. The two must work together.

Mercy and Healing

When we grasp the proper relationship between justice and mercy, we can begin to see the role mercy plays in healing our wounds caused by sin. The power of God's mercy to heal should never be underestimated. For those who receive it, God's mercy is mighty. It can bring about conversions, restoration, signs and miracles, reconciliation, peace, and restored hope.

Mercy is a force beyond our imagination. It is more powerful that an infinity of nuclear explosions, gentler than a baby's smile, more intimate that a young couple's first kiss, and more tender than a sleeping child in his mother's arms.

But these wondrous qualities of mercy only work if we allow them to. We have to be willing to accept God's mercy and the healing that comes with it. It is an open font available to anyone, especially the most fallen and sinful among us, assuming our hearts are not too hardened to accept it. We see this truth displayed in the Gospels.

On one occasion, a Pharisee named Simon invited Jesus to dinner (Lk 7:36–50). As he was there, reclining at the table and eating dinner, a sinful woman in the area learned of the Lord's presence. She went to Simon's home with a jar of perfume. When she approached, she sat at Christ's feet and anointed him with her tears, then wiped his feet with her hair, kissed them, and poured out her perfume.

Regrettably, the host of the dinner could not see the tender act of kindness and repentance. He only saw a sinner. The Gospel tells us, "Now when the Pharisee who had invited him saw it, he said to himself, 'If this man were a prophet, he would have known who and what sort of woman this is who is touching him, for she is a sinner'" (Lk 7:39).

Just as our culture is quick to define and identify themselves by their worst sins, so was Simon the Pharisee. But the Lord Jesus saw something more. He knew of the woman's sins, but he saw her as one of his own. She was more than just her sins and the Lord wanted her free and healed from the darkness and harm.

The rest of the scene plays out as follows, with Jesus saying:

> "A certain creditor had two debtors; one owed five hundred denarii, and the other fifty. When they could not pay, he forgave them both. Now which of them will love him more?" Simon answered, "The one, I suppose, to whom he forgave more." And he said to him, "You have judged rightly." Then turning toward the woman he said to Simon, "Do you see this woman? I entered your house, you gave me no water for my feet, but she has wet my feet with her tears and wiped them with her hair. You gave me no

kiss, but from the time I came in she has not ceased to kiss my feet. You did not anoint my head with oil, but she anointed my feet with ointment. Therefore I tell you, her sins, which are many, are forgiven, for she loved much; but he who is forgiven little, loves little." And he said to her, "Your sins are forgiven." Then those who were at table with him began to say among themselves, "Who is this, who even forgives sins?" And he said to the woman, "Your faith has saved you; go in peace." (Lk 7:41–50)

All things considered in the culture of that day, the sinful woman would have been the less likely to receive such abundant love, care, and affection from the Lord, and yet this is exactly how God works. He gives his mercy to everyone, even those who seem far removed from its possibility. The Lord desires to forgive and heal. He desires to give us all a fresh start, a spiritual reboot, perpetual new beginnings!

The beauty and power of God's mercy and healing can be heard and felt in the absolution of the sacrament of Penance, or Reconciliation. Popularly known as "confession," the sacrament has a sacred prayer offered by the priest. Sitting in the person of Christ, and serving as his instrument, the priest offers this prayer: "God, the Father of mercies, through the death and resurrection of his Son has reconciled the world to himself and sent the Holy Spirit among us for the forgiveness of sins; through the ministry of the Church may God give you pardon and peace, and I absolve you from your sins in the name of the Father, and of the Son, and of the Holy Spirit."

These are some of the holiest and most powerful words ever spoken on earth. They contain all the substance and depth of God's movement toward us for mercy and healing.

These anointed words remove sin by God's authority, they grant pardon, and they bestow graces of peace. This is the work of God. This is the mercy and healing he desires to bestow upon us in this life.

Living as We Pray

In receiving God's mercy, we are strengthened to give this mercy to others, and reciprocally, as we saw at the beginning of this chapter, we ask God to forgive us *as we* we forgive others.

To help demonstrate this, the Lord Jesus gave us the parable of the unforgiving servant (Mt 18:21–35). In this story, we see mercy being given to a servant who refused to give the same mercy to a fellow servant. When the master was told, the servant was severely punished, as the master told him, "You wicked servant! I forgave you all that debt because you pleaded with me; and should not you have had mercy on your fellow servant, as I had mercy on you?" (Mt 18:32–33).

In our lives as the children of God, we have to understand that our call to both receive and to give mercy are two sides of the same coin. St. Paul emphasizes this point, as he teaches us, "All this is from God, who through Christ reconciled us to himself and gave us the ministry of reconciliation; that is, in Christ God was reconciling the world to himself, not counting their trespasses against them, and entrusting to us the message of reconciliation. So we are ambassadors for Christ, God making his appeal through us. We beg you on behalf of Christ, be reconciled to God" (2 Cor 5:18–20).

And so, we have received this ministry of reconciliation as the adopted children of God, who are the recipients of his mercy and love. As we move throughout our lives and see evil, darkness, and desolation, we are called to carry the message of goodness, mercy, and hope. In order for us to do this well, we need to regularly avail ourselves of God's mercy. We need to frequently confess our sins, be healed, and receive the help of God's grace.

No one can be free or happy while holding resentment or anger in their hearts. In order for us, and others, to be happy, we must live a life of mercy. Admittedly, true forgiveness involves suffering, and compassion requires emotional strength to toss aside pride, anger, and self-pity. In this suffering for mercy, however, we suffer in the saving work of Christ.

In this way, we extend mercy to others, along with the freedom and healing that come with mercy. As such, we become instruments of grace and, through us, hope and peace are brought into marriages, families, friendships, workplaces, neighborhoods, parishes, cities, and entire nations.

If we are bold enough to seek mercy and share it with others, then mercy will triumph and new beginnings will be given.

In our world today, there are many general examples of how others have lived out the tenet of God's mercy contained in the Lord's Prayer. Here are just a few:

- Two neighbors who have a fight and one of them decides to swallow his pride and extend the hand of repentance and reconciliation.

- The newly married couple struggling to surrender their habits who offer a dozen acts of mercy and kindness every day to one another as they accustom themselves to their new life.

- The business person who realizes it's been a few years since his last confession and stops a priest at an airport asking if he could go to confession.

- The relatives who acknowledge that they have not truly forgiven a family member in their heart and begin to ask God for the grace of true mercy.

- The young adult fallen into dark habits who decides to regularly go to confession and fight for virtue and healthier living.

In each of these cases and more, we see an active effort to receive and share the mercy of God.

Examination of Conscience

- Do I trust in God's mercy and nurture a life of hope based on that mercy?

- Do I regularly go to confession, repenting of my sins and asking God's mercy?

- When I go to confession, do I take the time to examine my conscience well, or do I rush through a preparation for the sacrament?

- Do I name my specific sins in confession, or do I purposely broaden or disguise them?

- Do I encourage those under my care to regularly go to confession? If a parent, do I regularly take my children to the sacrament?

- Do I exercise humility for apologizing or asking for forgiveness when I have caused hurt or harm to another person?

- Do I generously give mercy to others?

- Do I give mercy to others, even when they don't ask for it or seem unrepentant?

- Do I make reasonable excuses for the shortcomings of others?

- Have I indulged dark spirits of self-pity, anger, resentment, or bitterness towards others?

- Do I surround myself with entertainment that fuels a culture of unforgiveness, vengeance, and violence?

School of Discipleship

Continuing in our School of Discipleship, it is now time to look at the fifth tenet of the Lord's Prayer: **Forgive us our trespasses, as we forgive those who trespass against us.**

When we show mercy to others, the Holy Spirit bestows us with the gift of **counsel.** Mercy cultivates within us a compassionate and loving spirit. If we offer mercy to someone who is suffering, whether it be physical, emotional, or spiritual, we are able to bring them counsel and make them feel better. Just as we may guide a person away from sin or instruct them on how to deal with emotional traumas, so the Holy Spirit, in fulfilling the promise of this tenet of the Lord's Prayer, will give us mercy and bless us with the gift of counsel, which enlightens us to do and say the right thing in the face of trials.

Once we receive this gift, the virtue of **prudence** is perfected in our soul. As we engage the hearts of others through counsel, we are led to prudently accompany our neighbor. The counsel we take in from the Holy Spirit allows us to act prudently; or said in another way, it enables us to be careful in our decisions and in what we say. The *Catechism* says prudence is "the virtue that disposes practical reason to discern our true good in every circumstance and to choose the right means of achieving it" (CCC 1806).

This tenet of the Lord's Prayer, gift, and virtue help us to better understand the beatitude **"Blessed are they who show mercy, mercy shall be theirs."** This bears a clear connection to acting with mercy and being shown mercy, as forgiveness goes hand in hand with mercy. The blossoming of this beatitude leads us to the promise that we will be given mercy. If we show mercy to others, we will be the beneficiary of God's mercy.

Lastly, the path that begins with this tenet of the Lord's Prayer and crosses through these other aspects of the spiritual life helps us to recognize the hoarding and darkness of the capital sin of **greed**. One might think that the opposite of mercy is anger or envy, and while these vices are opposed to mercy, the actual opposite of mercy is greed. With greed, we usually think in materialistic terms; we think of someone of great wealth or of some Wall Street tycoon. But greed can be seen principally in the context of our emotions and the movements of our hearts. Mercy is about being completely selfless, open, and free, whereas greed is self-absorbed, closed-in, and enslaved to its passions, emotions, and desires.

The person entrenched in greed is focused more on their own importance than on a genuine openness and care of others. A greedy person will not share happiness, love, or mercy. He will stay angry over an offense and burden the happiness of others. Greed relishes in grudges and digs deeper pits of animosity toward others. It cannot let go of a hurt

and bounces between resentment and self-pity on the one
hand and manipulation and deception on the other. Just as
the material greed of the Wall Street tycoon wants to collect
as much worldly treasure as possible, so the spiritually greedy
person wants to collect grudges and animosity and store them
up in a bank of ill-will.

Those trapped in greed become strangers to themselves.
They pity the poor but do not offer any assistance. They judge
offenses but never ask for forgiveness. They envy the happy
but don't seek happiness themselves. As greed desperately
seeks to hoard, it only empties our hearts even more. Left to
its own devices, greed will black out the light of goodness in
our hearts and lead us down a path of misery, bitterness, and
hatred.

As the promise of the merciful is to receive mercy, so the
punishment of greed is an empty and bitter heart. The greedy
person who collects earthly wealth and does not share it will
not be given charity if he loses all that he has; in the same
way, one who does not offer mercy will not receive it himself
when he is in need.

In conclusion, the fifth row of our spiritual matrix looks
like this:

TENET OF THE LORD'S PRAYER	GIFT OF THE HOLY SPIRIT	CORRESPONDING VIRTUE	BEATITUDE	CAPITAL SIN
Forgive us our trespasses as we forgive those who trespass against us.	Counsel	Prudence	Blessed are the merciful, for they shall obtain mercy.	Greed

Prayer

Heavenly Father,
You pour out your loving kindness on all your children.
You draw close to all who turn to you.
You graciously bestow your mercy on all who seek it.
Help me to be free from sin,
and to live in the freedom of your children.
Strengthen me in my hurts and sufferings.
Guide me in giving your mercy to others.
Show me your path of peace.
Through Christ our Lord.
Amen.

Three Truths on Mercy:

+ God offers his mercy and loving kindness to all his children.
+ God's mercy is a powerful force that brings healing, hope, and new beginnings.
+ As we receive God's mercy, we are called to give mercy to others.

The Lord's Mercy:

"But finding no way to bring him in, because of the crowd, they went up on the roof and let him down with his bed through the tiles into their midst before Jesus. And when he saw their faith he said, 'Man, your sins are forgiven you.'"

Luke 5:19–20

Seventy-Seven Times:

"Then Peter came up and said to him, 'Lord, how often shall my brother sin against me, and I forgive him? As many as seven times?' Jesus said to him, 'I do not say to you seven times, but seventy times seven.'"

Matthew 18:21–22

Mercy Prayer
Eternal Father,
I offer you the Body and Blood,
Soul and Divinity
of your Dearly Beloved Son,
Our Lord, Jesus Christ,
in atonement for our sins
and those of the whole world.
Amen.

Additional Reading:

If you'd like to know more about God's mercy, this book can help:

Jeffrey Kirby and Brian Kennelly, *Doors of Mercy: A Journey through Salvation History* (Saint Benedict Press, 2016).

If you'd like to know more about our call to mercy, this book on Saint Maria Goretti can help:

Jeffrey Kirby, *The Life and Witness of Saint Maria Goretti: Our Little Saint of the Beatitudes* (TAN Books, 2015).

CHAPTER 7

Lead Us

And lead us not into temptation.

MATTHEW 6:13

Leading Us

The fifth tenet of the Lord's Prayer, "forgive us our trespasses as we forgive those who trespass against us," is followed by the sixth tenet: "And lead us not into temptation." And so, we petition God for his protection and guidance. This chapter will now focus on the sixth tenet of the Lord's Prayer.

One Day

Some years ago, I served as the vicar of vocations for my diocese. As such, it was my privilege and responsibility to accompany and help young men to figure out God's will for their lives. Early into this specialized ministry, I realized that many of the young men were attempting to discern God's will, but they didn't really know God or the extent of his ways. In response to this observation, my office established

113

discipleship groups. Working closely with local pastors, high school chaplains, university campus ministers, and youth ministers, discipleship groups were formed throughout the diocese that met monthly or even weekly.

Building on the regular curriculum of the various schools or campus ministries, the groups focused on the sacraments, prayer, virtue, and holy fellowship. The meetings were meant to give a crash course in discipleship with practical wisdom and applicable steps to grow in holiness. The mottos of the groups were simple: "Discipleship before Discernment" and "Believing needs Belonging." These simple mottos summarized these truths: We all have to learn how to follow before we could know the ways of God, and no Christian is meant to be a disciple by himself. We all need each other if we are going to persevere and flourish in our faith and discipleship.

The groups were surprisingly successful, and many young men regularly attended the meetings. In time, a culture developed among the members of the different groups and spiritual topics were discussed in an open and unabashed spirit. Of course, some of the young men insisted they weren't discerning the priesthood and were just there to learn about God. Others began to ask for spiritual direction, and so schedules were set up every month before and after meetings.

On one occasion, while I was meeting with a regular member of one of the groups, the young man joined me in prayer. When the prayer ended, he made the sign of the cross, looked up, and said with a huge smile, "Father, it's been one day!"

"What do you mean?" I asked.

"Father, since I was in middle school, I've been looking at pornography. When I got my first cell phone, it got a lot worse. In high school, I didn't hang out with friends because

I was looking at so much porn. And every girl I looked at, I compared to the women in the videos. It was hard to control my thoughts. And when I started college, it got really bad."

The young man continued with a spiraling narrative, full of lust, self-centeredness, and loneliness. He described viewing pornography multiple times a day and habitually committing sexual sins relating to it. He even looked at porn on his way to class. The young man was a slave to his darker passions and was led by a raw desire for arousal and pleasure.

In the course of attending the discipleship group, however, he started to apply ascetical practices to fortify his will by grace. He set boundaries against occasions of sin, fought against internally objectifying other people, adjusted his use of electronics, and spent more time with *real* people in wholesome and edifying interactions. All of these hard-fought efforts pointed to our meeting and to his declaration, "It's been one day!" Yes, he reached the point where he was sober from pornography for an entire day!

Now, this might not seem like a huge accomplishment to some people, but for this young person, it was a monumental achievement. He concluded his powerful testimony by saying, "Father, all this stuff really works. God comes through. I can really get out of all this junk!"

The day's sobriety from pornography was a reflection of the victory of grace over sin. It was a clear sign to this young Christian that God will lead us out of temptation if we turn to him, rely on him, cooperate with his grace, and follow him wherever he leads us.

Admittedly, the young man still had a long way to go, and I was able to help him find a good counselor and support group to further his efforts to stay sexually pure. But his initial efforts gave him hope. They showed him that he was not alone in the darkness and that there was a way out of it. He learned, as we all have in different ways, that God is with us and leads us not into temptation but into the ways of truth, goodness, and holiness.

In our lives, as we struggle with sin, do we realize that God seeks to lead us out of darkness and into his own wonderful light? Are we open and willing to abandon sinful ways and follow God wherever he leads us?

Clarification of Meaning

This sixth tenet of the Lord's Prayer is an urgent petition. It expresses our critical need for our heavenly Father and the help of his grace. It acknowledges our vulnerability and helplessness in the face of evil and temptation, and it directs our hearts to the source of all strength and power.

Yet as we look at the wording of this sixth tenet, we might become confused. We pray, "Lead us not into temptation." Would God ever truly lead us into temptation? Isn't that contrary to his kindness toward us?

In the face of such questions, the *Catechism of the Catholic Church* provides clarity. The Greek language, in which the New Testament was written, is an incredibly rich language with a breadth of meaning contained in simple, single words. When it comes to the Lord's Prayer, and especially this sixth tenet, we hit a difficulty with Greek. The Greek word for "lead" is incredibly difficult to translate into a single English word. As the *Catechism* points out, the Greek word means both "do not allow us to enter into temptation" and "do not let us yield to temptation" (CCC 2846). With this clarification, we can understand what the Lord is actually teaching us and what we are actually requesting of our Father.

In the end, we're asking our heavenly Father to liberate us from our slavery to sin, guard us against our weaknesses, empower us against our inclinations to evil, protect us against the darkness of our world, and be our safeguard and companion along the path of righteousness.

As we've already seen throughout the explanation of the other tenets of the Lord's Prayer, our world and our human nature are fallen. In its fall from grace, creation entered a time of both anguish amidst darkness and of expectation toward redemption. The Lord Jesus expressed it in this way: "When a woman is in labor, she has pain, because her hour has come; but when she is delivered of the child, she no longer remembers the anguish, for joy that a child is born into the world. So you have sorrow now, but I will see you again and your hearts will rejoice, and no one will take your joy from you" (Jn 16:21–22).

Like a woman in labor, therefore, we await the revelation of God's kingdom and glory. We await our redemption. The Lord Jesus, our older brother, has vanquished the fallen kingdom of sin and darkness. We, his siblings by adoption, are the recipients of his grace and are called to be his instruments and to dispel the darkness in our hearts and in our world. We are summoned to transform our world and to fight so that good can triumph over evil.

In this effort, we realize that we too are weak and broken, and so we cry out, "Lead us not into temptation." We cry out, "Lord God, help us!" And when our journey on this earth is done, we say with the Lord Jesus, "Father, into your hands I commit my spirit" (Lk 23:46).

The Lord's Example

Throughout his life and ministry, the Lord Jesus called evil for what it was. He named the prince of this world and declared his opposition to his fallen kingdom (cf. Jn 14:30). He would enter the battle for the sake of righteousness and suffer its agony on our behalf.

At the very beginning of his ministry, Jesus accepted baptism from his precursor, St. John the Baptist. After he was baptized, God the Father announced from the heavens, "This is my beloved Son, with whom I am well pleased" (Mt 3:17). After this powerful moment, Jesus went into the desert to prepare himself for his mission. There, he encountered the evil one, who said to him, "If you are the Son of God . . ." and three temptations followed (cf. Mt 4:1–11).

But wait, something was missing! Again, it was subtle. When God the Father spoke, he said "beloved Son"; when the evil one spoke, he deviously dropped "beloved" and simply spoke of "son." It was a purposeful act, a strategy of manipulation. As the devil moved forward and waged his temptations, he wanted Jesus to feel alone. He wanted Jesus to rely on his own strength rather than on the divine fellowship and favor of God. Inherently, he was telling the Lord Jesus, you are not "beloved," you are not protected, you are by yourself. The evil one relied on these lies as he mounted his attack, which culminated in the ultimate suggestion of betrayal: "Again, the devil took him to a very high mountain, and showed him all the kingdoms of the world and the glory of them; and he said to him, 'All these I will give you, if you will fall down and worship me'" (Mt 4:8–9).

Jesus stood his ground and was not led into temptation.

He denounced the evil one, declaring, "Begone, Satan! for it is written, 'You shall worship the Lord your God and him only shall you serve'" (Mt 4:10).

The Lord turned to the Father and relied on his divine communion and commission. He knew the Father was with him and would not betray him. The Father was a strength to him.

It's no accident that the Lord's public ministry is marked by multiple exorcisms and denunciations of bad spirits. The entire force of evil, the impulse behind destruction and deception, was in league against him. And yet, the Lord Jesus—true God and true Man—stayed the course. He prayed to the Father, appealing to his goodness. He allowed himself to be dependent on the Father's care and guidance. The two were in close union, with the Lord's human nature obeying and seeking the direction of God the Father. As the *Letter to the Hebrews* explains, "In the days of his flesh, Jesus offered up prayers and supplications, with loud cries and tears, to him who was able to save him from death, and he was heard for his godly fear. Although he was a Son, he learned obedience through what he suffered; and being made perfect he became the source of eternal salvation to all who obey him, being designated by God a high priest according to the order of Melchizedek" (Heb 5:7–10).

In these ways, Jesus trusted in the presence and providence of God the Father. As such, he could endure suffering, accept persecution, and persevere in his mission. In his high priestly prayer in the Upper Room, the Lord said to the Father: "Glorify your Son that the Son may glorify you.... I glorified you on earth, having accomplished the work which you gave me to do" (Jn 17:1, 4).

The Lord's work of redemption culminated in his paschal mystery, which is his passion, death, and resurrection. The paschal mystery is the definitive battle between good and evil, light and darkness, God's redemption and the evil one's damnation. And Jesus came ready for the fight. In the Garden of Gethsemane, he asked that the cup of suffering might pass, but above such desires, he sought nothing else but complete union with the Father and a total submission to his will (cf. Mt 26:39). The Lord allowed himself in all things—even in the throes of betrayal, mockery, and torture—to be led, not into temptation, but into the loving kindness of God the Father. He would not run away. He would learn obedience through suffering.

Battle and Agony

Choosing not to succumb to sin and darkness, we are called to take up the mantle of the Lord Jesus and become a part of his battle for the redemption of the world. In taking his side, we enter into a battle between "the flesh and spirit." St. Paul vividly describes this battle:

> But I say, walk by the Spirit, and do not gratify the desires of the flesh. For the desires of the flesh are against the Spirit, and the desires of the Spirit are against the flesh; for these are opposed to each other, to prevent you from doing what you would.
>
> But if you are led by the Spirit you are not under the law. Now the works of the flesh are plain: fornication, impurity, licentiousness, idolatry, sorcery, enmity, strife, jealousy, anger, selfishness, dissension, party spirit, envy, drunkenness, carousing, and the like.

I warn you, as I warned you before, that those who do such things shall not inherit the kingdom of God. But the fruit of the Spirit is love, joy, peace, patience, kindness, goodness, faithfulness, gentleness, self-control; against such there is no law. And those who belong to Christ Jesus have crucified the flesh with its passions and desires. If we live by the Spirit, let us also walk by the Spirit. (Gal 5:16–25)

As we use these terms, it's helpful to clarify what they mean. For example, *spirit* is a reference to the working of the Holy Spirit in our lives. It summarizes our desire for God and the workings of his grace. Additionally, in this context, the expression "the flesh" is not a reference to the body. While there are times in the Bible when the word *flesh* is synonymous with our physical bodies, there are other times when it is speaking of something else.

Whenever the word *flesh* is preceded by the definite article *the*, the term means something much broader and much more sinister. When "the flesh" is cited, it's a reference to the disordered parts of our souls. It's pinpointing our unruly desire to rebel against God and his goodness. It's a naming of our wayward and self-centered passions that follow no sense of reason or virtue. "The flesh" seeks nothing but its own pleasure and satisfaction. It's a synonym for concupiscence and is an unchecked and defiant impulse towards ourselves and our lusts for power, vainglory, and sexual enjoyment.

As we indulge the flesh, we lose an awareness of ourselves. We follow lost paths, build shaky foundations on sand, create ungovernable cities, submit to the kingdom of darkness, and propagate a culture of death. St. Paul summarizes these consequences: "For those who live according to the flesh set their minds on things of the flesh, but those who live according to the Spirit set their minds on the things of the Spirit" (Rom 8:5).

And so, our battle is against the flesh, our disordered desires. It's an agony we accept within our own hearts and within our world. The Spirit battles to allow goodness to triumph. We are invited to be a part of this campaign. This means that we accept temptation. We know that it will be a part of our lives and so we ask God to preserve us from it or to give us his power to overcome it.

Temptation, therefore, becomes a testing and a trial. It's the crucible of the kingdom since it involves our hearts, our loves, and our decisions. Our avoidance or victory over temptations molds and shapes who we are and helps us to show the glory of God's goodness and the splendor of his holiness. In short, it makes us stronger so that we can better prevail in battle.

Living as We Pray

In our fight for goodness and holiness, we will endure distractions and temptations of every kind. There will be times when temptations seem overwhelming and impossible to resist. Whether these temptations are against charity, humility, purity, generosity, or peace, they will be real, intense, and unavoidable. The fallen world will call to us in these moments of temptation and tell us to "take it easy" and just submit to sin.

Temptation surrounds the horror of sin in seductive wrappings and supposedly noble intentions. It will manipulate, lie, change the rules, make lofty promises, ensure secrecy, cloud our judgments, corrode our wills, and seduce our human desires. Temptation doesn't play fair. It's not reasonable and refuses to follow logic or principles of fairness. It has only one goal: the slavery of God's adopted children to sin and their captivity for evil and darkness.

What are we to do in the face of such temptation?

We claim our status as the adopted children of God. We remind ourselves that no temptation is greater than God's grace and that our Father will not allow any temptation beyond our abilities (cf. 1 Cor 10:13). In reclaiming our identity in the midst of temptations, we move forward and follow the example of the Lord Jesus. We suffer, we hope, we fight, we love, we watch, we persevere, and we trust. We pray with our older brother: "And lead us not into temptation."

In our battles against temptation, we are reminded:

It is for discipline that you have to endure. God is treating you as sons; for what son is there whom his father does not discipline? If you are left without discipline, in which all have participated, then you are illegitimate children and not sons.

Besides this, we have had earthly fathers to discipline us and we respected them. Shall we not much more be subject to the Father of spirits and live? For they disciplined us for a short time at their pleasure, but he disciplines us for our good, that we may share his holiness.

For the moment all discipline seems painful rather than pleasant; later it yields the peaceful fruit of righteousness to those who have been trained by it. Therefore lift your drooping hands and strengthen your weak knees, and make straight paths for your feet, so that what is lame may not be put out of joint but rather be healed. (Heb 12:7–13)

And so, our temptations are opportunities to prove our love for God and our neighbor, grow in righteousness, be freed from false attachments and allurements, and be strengthened in goodness. They are a discipline from our loving Father and a means for us to vanquish the kingdom of sin.

In our world today, there are many examples of how others have fought temptation and lived out this tenet of the Lord's Prayer. Here are just a few:

- The married man who distances himself from the flirtatiousness of a colleague because he loves his wife and doesn't want anything to diminish his affection and respect for her.

- The newly married couple who struggles to follow Natural Family Planning and is tempted to use birth control but remains faithful to biblical teachings on sexual intimacy.

- The businessman tempted to cheat on a contract and overcharge but dies to his greed and remains honest.

- The teenager tempted to imitate his friends who disrespect their parents but instead fills his heart with gratitude and respect for them.

- The person who has committed a grave sin and is tempted to avoid the sacrament of confession but instead truly repents and goes to confession as soon as possible.

In each of these cases and more, we see an active effort to fight temptation and avoid sin.

Examination of Conscience

- Do I pray every day and ask God for his guidance and protection?

- Am I honest with myself and others about my strengths and weaknesses?

- Do I regularly examine my conscience and scrutinize my life according to the teachings of the Lord Jesus?

- Do I frequently go to confession and seek the grace of the sacrament as a help in avoiding or fighting temptation?

- Do I avoid occasions of sin or personal weakness?

- Do I use the ascetical practices of the Church, such as fasting, abstinence, abnegations, and devotional exercises, as a help to fighting temptation and persevering in virtue?

- Do I seek out holy fellowship as a help in avoiding or fighting against temptation?

- Do I generously offer up my sufferings against temptation for the good of others?

- Do I avoid entertainment (movies, songs, magazines, etc.) that fuel or enhance temptations?

- Do I voice an opposition to public events, places, or monies that are used for evil purposes?

School of Discipleship

Continuing in our School of Discipleship, it is now time to look at the sixth tenet of the Lord's Prayer: **And lead us not into temptation.**

As we try to nurture an open heart to God's guidance, the Holy Spirit bestows us with the gift of **understanding**. When we understand something, we have transparency—meaning, it is clear to us. As the promise of God's help is given to us, those who implore God's help will see God and his divine providence—meaning, they will have complete clarity concerning his will for their lives and for the world.

Once we receive this gift, the virtue of **faith** is perfected in our soul. The *Catechism* says faith is "the virtue by which we believe in God and believe all that he has said and revealed to us. . . . For this reason the believer seeks to know and do God's will" (CCC 1814). In gaining clarity for God's will, our faith is strengthened because we see his plan and purpose for our lives, and those with a strong faith are the ones who will see God.

This tenet of the Lord's Prayer, gift, and virtue help us to better understand the beatitude **"Blessed are the pure in heart, for they shall see God."** Faith and understanding help us to see the scope of evil, the intentions of the wicked, and the occasions of sin. When received and exercised well, they can help us persevere in our struggle to obtain a pure heart. The blossoming of this petition is the promise of this beatitude, which is to see God. If we are led "not into temptation," then we are led instead to God.

Lastly, the path that begins with this tenet of the Lord's Prayer and crosses through these other aspects of the spiritual life helps us to recognize the foul and self-centered nature of the capital sin of **lust**. It should not surprise us that this is the opposite of those who seek to be led by God and to see him through a pure heart. The person enslaved to lust is absorbed in himself and cannot understand the needs or dignity of others. He has no clarity concerning God's will because he is blinded by his passions and his faith is weakened by his sins.

Seeking a pure heart is to desire faithfulness in our lives, with our feelings, thoughts, words, and actions. It shows a trust in God, a docility to goodness, a love for neighbor, and a chastity of mind and body.

Lust is the opposite. It craves pleasure in a disordered and immoral way. It longs for euphoria, highs, and self-indulgence. Lust cares for nothing other than its own pursuit of gratification and appeasement. When entertained, lust consumes the person. Other people become mere objects of pleasure or utility. The ability to experience transcendence or seek the providence of God becomes blurred and shady.

As the promise of those who seek God's direction is a pure heart, so the punishment of lust is to be blinded by our passions and be led into temptation and away from God.

In conclusion, the sixth row of our spiritual matrix looks like this:

TENET OF THE LORD'S PRAYER	GIFT OF THE HOLY SPIRIT	CORRESPONDING VIRTUE	BEATITUDE	CAPITAL SIN
And lead us not into Temptation.	Understanding	Faith	Blessed are the pure in heart, for they shall see God.	Lust

Prayer

Heavenly Father,
You are our Good Shepherd and Mighty Companion,
Guide us and direct us according to your goodness.
Lead us along the path of your loving kindness.
Dispel the darkness and scatter the evil around us.

Draw close to us. Strengthen us.
Help us to live as your children.
Through Christ our Lord.
Amen.

Three Truths on Being Led by God:

+ God created all things beautiful and good.
+ While still good, creation and human nature are fallen and inclined to darkness.
+ God is ever-present and willing to lead us along the path of righteousness.

The Psalmist's Prayer

"The LORD is my shepherd, I shall not want;
he makes me lie down in green pastures.
He leads me beside still waters,
he restores my soul.
He leads me in paths of righteousness
for his name's sake.
Even though I walk through the valley of the
shadow of death,
I fear no evil;
for you are with me;
your rod and your staff,
they comfort me."

Psalm 23:1–4

The Father's Care

"What man of you, if his son asks him for bread, will give him a stone? Or if he asks for a fish, will give him a serpent? If you, then, who are evil, know how to give good gifts to your children, how much more will your Father who is in heaven give good things to those who ask him!"

Matthew 7:9–11

The Faithfulness of God

"No temptation has overtaken you that is not common to man. God is faithful, and he will not let you be tempted beyond your strength, but with the temptation will also provide the way of escape, that you may be able to endure it."

1 Corinthians 10:13

Suscipe Prayer

Take Lord, and receive all my liberty,
my memory, my understanding,
and my entire will,
all that I have and possess.
You have given all to me.
To you, oh Lord, I return it.
All is yours,
dispose of it wholly according to your will.
Give me your love and your grace,
for this is sufficient for me.
Amen.

Additional Reading:

If you'd like to know more about Christian discipleship and the battle for holiness, this book can help:

Jeffrey Kirby, *Lord, Teach Us to Pray: A Guide to the Spiritual Life and Christian Discipleship* (Saint Benedict Press, 2014).

CHAPTER 8

Deliver Us

But deliver us from evil.

MATTHEW 6:13

Delivering Us

The sixth tenet of the Lord's Prayer, "And lead us not into temptation," is followed by the seventh tenet: "But deliver us from evil." This seventh tenet concludes the second portion of the Lord's Prayer. The four tenets of this second portion involved supplications, "Give us," "Forgive us," "Lead us," and "Deliver us." In this last tenet, which concludes the great prayer of the Lord Jesus, we petition God for his shelter and security. This chapter will now focus on the seventh tenet of the Lord's Prayer.

"Behold, the Lamb of God"

While in the seminary at the Pontifical North American College, I was blessed to meet, hear, and read about many of the heroes of our Faith. It seemed like every religious order,

ecclesial movement, universal apostolate, cause for canoniza-
tion, and pious association of the faithful found themselves
hosting some event in Rome. I suppose it is true that all roads
lead there!

One perk was that, as an extension of these various events,
seminarians got a lot of free stuff, especially books and devotional items. On one occasion, I stumbled into a conference
on clergy in the World War II era. I wasn't expecting to sit
through the event, but the wartime testimonies and witnesses
of several Catholic priests caught my attention. I ended up
attending most of the event (and missing a few classes because
of it). During the accounts of one priest, I heard the following
story.

There was a priest offering Mass at the main altar of his
church in one of the war-torn areas. At the time, he would
have been facing the tabernacle for the Eucharistic Sacrifice.
When he reached the Eucharistic Prayer and Consecration,
he said "all hell broke loose" behind him. But being in the
midst of the sacrifice, he continued and devoutly paid attention to the Real Presence of the Lord before him. He heard
blasts, screaming, explosions, structures falling, howls, and crying. But the priest stayed focused and moved along with the
Mass.

When it came time for him to turn to the congregation to present the Lord's Presence, he explained, "I took
the Host and prepared it as usual, I turned to present the
Blessed Sacrament to the people, and as I turned, I saw nothing. Everything was gone. The entire church beyond the altar
area was gone, buildings were demolished throughout the
neighborhood, everything was leveled. Everything was completely gone. While the Mass was being offered, bombs had

been dropped by aircraft, hit the district, and there was total annihilation."

Then, as he explained it, the priest realized the Lord Jesus—truly present in the Eucharist—was in his hands and that he was still within the sacred sacrifice. He came to his senses and continued the Mass. He raised the Host, as the directions of the Mass proscribed, held it for a moment, and then announced with all his heart:"Behold, the Lamb of God, behold him who takes away the sins of the world."

These words, always so powerful, were exactly what was needed at that moment. In the midst of unspeakable suffering and total destruction, the Lamb of God was raised up and declared the Savior—our deliverer—and our only hope.

Do we cry out to God for deliverance when we see or experience evil? Do we acknowledge God as our deliverer and rely on him? Do we look to God for hope and perseverance?

Evil and the evil one

There is debate over the exact wording of this last tenet. Is the Greek better translated as "evil" or as "the evil one"? While theologians and linguists debate the question, Pope Benedict XVI gives us a clear path to follow as he soberly observes,"The two are ultimately inseparable." In saying this, the beloved pontiff is pointing out that "evil" (in the singular) denotes the kingdom of sin, rather than "evils" (in the plural) which denote specific sinful acts. As such, the kingdom of evil is ruled by its prince, the evil one (cf. Jn 14:30). And so, evil and the evil one are inseparable and both perspectives can help us to understand this last tenet of the Lord's Prayer.

By naming the evil one, we are acknowledging that he is

not an abstraction *but a real being*, with a real personhood and
with real power and influence. This fallen angel, called Lucifer,
the devil, and Satan, hates God and has declared himself an
enemy to creation and to the human family. He desires nothing else but our damnation and destruction. The devil dances
when we destroy ourselves. Satan sings as we sin without
restraint. And Lucifer laughs when we lose grace and linger
in darkness. He is evil, and he seeks nothing but our misery.

St. John records the Lord's words about the evil one in his
Gospel, "He was a murderer from the beginning, not holding
to the truth, for there is no truth in him. When he lies, he
speaks his native language, for he is a liar and the father of
lies" (Jn 8:44).

This is our enemy, and he is cunning, sly, and ruthless. He
has created a false kingdom in our world and tyrannically rules
it and callously seeks to spread it. This dark kingdom fuels raw
power, justifies greed, objectifies people, rewards immorality,
and instigates division and accusation. It promotes lies and
seeks the annihilation of human dignity and the goodness of
creation.

This is the shadow kingdom of the glorious kingdom of
our heavenly Father. And it is precisely from this kingdom,
and its deception and darkness, that we beg our heavenly
Father's deliverance every day: "But deliver us from evil!"

In the Thick of the Struggle

As God's beloved children, we have been formed by the other
truths contained in the Lord's Prayer and have been led to
this last tenet seeking deliverance. We know that the kingdom
of sin is foreign to the kingdom of our Father. We know that

we, and our world, have been created for far greater and more glorious things than sin and deception. We know that our inheritance is a kingdom of truth, light, goodness, and peace. The reality of these two kingdoms doesn't come as a surprise to us.

St. John summarizes our state of affairs in his first letter: "We know that any one born of God does not sin, but He who was born of God keeps him, and the evil one does not touch him. We know that we are of God, and the whole world is in the power of the evil one" (1 Jn 5:18–19).

As such, this last tenet of the Lord's Prayer is specifically the petition of the child of God who is "all in," who has said yes to God, and who is willing to be in the thick of the struggle to bring about God's deliverance in our world today. This is the supplication of the person who wants our world liberated from the evil one and his false kingdom.

Living as We Pray

In our pining for God's deliverance in a fallen world, we are carried by the knowledge of God's love and of his care for us. It is the assurance of this love, and our desire to share it with others, that compels us to speak the truth, defend beauty, labor for peace, promote goodness, and selflessly serve others, even our adversaries and those who harm us.

In this way, the last tenet of the Lord's Prayer takes us back to its first three petitions, since our longing for deliverance from evil is ultimately yearning for the coming of God's kingdom, for an intimate union with his will, and for the universal glorification of his name.

St. Paul describes this thirsting and suffering for the sake of God's kingdom in chapter 8 of his letter to the Romans. The chapter is perhaps one of the most consoling portions of his entire collection of letters. In part, the great apostle tells us:

> If God is for us, who is against us? He who did not spare his own Son but gave him up for us all, will he not also give us all things with him? . . . Who shall separate us from the love of Christ? Shall tribulation, or distress, or persecution, or famine, or nakedness, or peril, or sword? . . . No, in all these things we are more than conquerors through him who loved us. For I am sure that neither death, nor life, nor angels, nor principalities, nor things present nor things to come, nor height, nor depth, nor anything else in all creation, will be able to separate us from the love of God in Christ Jesus our Lord. (Rom 8:31–39)

And in this great campaign for the sake of God's kingdom, we are consoled by the powerful prayer of the Lord Jesus to the Father, which he prayed on our behalf: "I do not pray that you should take them out of the world, but that you should keep them from the evil one" (Jn 17:15).

In our world today, there are many general examples of people who have sought out God's deliverance from evil. Here are just a few:

- The busy family who reaches out to the needy in their community.

- The lawyer who sees the injustice of the world and, rather than falling into despair, continues to fight for goodness and seeks to be an instrument of fairness.

- The social worker who experiences broken homes,

abuse, and neglect on a regular basis and yet retains a spirit of hope and perseverance.

- The teenager who realizes that the bullying of her friends is hurtful to others and tells them to stop while also befriending those who were bullied.

- The wife who cares for her husband as he's dying of cancer and knows that we were not meant to die and so asks God to welcome him into paradise.

In each of these cases and more, we see a zealous yearning for God's deliverance from all evil.

Examination of Conscience

- Do I actively entrust the sufferings and evils of my life and of the world to the Father in the Eucharistic Sacrifice?

- Do I speak to God from my heart about the suffering in my life and ask the help of his grace?

- Am I compassionate toward the sufferings and evils of those around me?

- Do I offer spiritual sacrifices for God's deliverance from evil in our world?

- Am I generous with my time to those who are in distress, suffering, or need encouragement?

- Do I serve the poor and sick?

- Do I know the people in my neighborhood? Am I attentive to their sufferings and needs?

- Am I active in my parish, my community, and in politics to help spread God's kingdom?

- Do I generously offer up my sufferings against temptation for the good of others?

- Do I engage in entertainment that promotes empathy and compassion towards others? Do I avoid entertainment that glorifies violence, sexual objectivity of others, raw power, and greed?

School of Discipleship

Continuing in our School of Discipleship, it is now time to look at the seventh tenet of the Lord's Prayer: **But deliver us from evil.**

If we seek God's deliverance from evil, the Holy Spirit will bestow upon us the gift of **wisdom.** A wise person understands God's providence. Wisdom helps him see earthly things in light of eternity, and in doing so, he nourishes a detachment from those earthly things. The wise person does not only value what profits him in this world but also greatly values the things that will get him to heaven, chiefly peace of soul. The wise person is at peace because of the knowledge he has of what really matters in life, and by extension, he spreads that peace to those around him. This is why so many wise people carry themselves with calm and peace.

Once we receive this gift, the virtue of **charity** is perfected in our soul, which is another word for love. The *Catechism* says charity is "the virtue by which we love God above all things for his own sake, and our neighbor as ourselves for the love of God" (CCC 1822). As we seek to know the heart of God and that of our neighbors through wisdom, we are brought into a broader horizon that allows us to live a more generous life of love and charity.

This tenet of the Lord's Prayer, gift, and virtue help us to better understand the beatitude **"Blessed are the peace-makers, for they shall be called sons of God"** since wisdom and charity help us to trust God, perceive his providential order, discern its guidance in our lives, and boldly follow him. The blossoming of this tenet is the promise of being called the children of God. If we are delivered from evil, delivered from being the children of the evil one, then we will truly become and live as the children of God.

Lastly, the path that begins with this tenet of the Lord's Prayer and crosses through these other aspects of the spiritual life helps us identify the tragedy and self-centeredness of the capital sin of **gluttony**. The life of a glutton is focused on himself and has very little room for anyone or for any other good thing. A glutton seeks to block peace since he obsesses, overindulges, and exaggerates one part of creation's order. Peace is marked by a sense of balance and harmony, whereas gluttony is identified by extremism and polarity.

The person bloated by gluttony cannot understand the needs or love of others. Such a person is stuck in a cesspool of his own passions and desires. He loves himself too much, taking in everything for himself, forfeiting a love of neighbor and a life of self-donation. The glutton consumes the world, while the one who seeks deliverance from God pours himself out into the world to make it a better (a more peaceful and ordered) place.

A glutton does not just pursue money, power, food, drink, or pleasure to satisfy a need or a legitimate want but will actually pursue these created goods beyond what is necessary or even healthy. His wants have no end. The glutton thinks only of himself. He does not care about the one who suffers because of his own craving for consolation. He does not want the poor to have food because he desires food only for himself and his enjoyment. The glutton does not want a sinner to undergo conversion because he wants the person to sin for him or his pleasure. The glutton cannot care about the things of God because he is only focused on his own divinization by usurping a height, fulfillment, or glory that properly belongs only to God.

The person who seeks deliverance from God forgives and works to conclude arguments, tension, or strike through truth, love, and selfless service. The glutton, however, feeds animosity and friction by selfishly demanding and insisting on his own favor, goals, rights, or desires.

The person who petitions God for deliverance sees the whole order of creation and is selfless. He is willing to sacrifice for the sake of others and the common good. By contrast, a glutton sacrifices the good of others to enhance his own prosperity.

As the promise of being a peacemaker is to be called a child of God, so the punishment of gluttony is to be only a child of himself (and thus, of the evil one) since he displays the ongoing self-centeredness and immaturity of a juvenile who never grows up and who never sees the greater world around him.

In conclusion, the seventh row of our spiritual matrix looks like this:

TENET OF THE LORD'S PRAYER	GIFT OF THE HOLY SPIRIT	CORRESPONDING VIRTUE	BEATITUDE	CAPITAL SIN
But deliver us from evil.	Wisdom	Charity	Blessed are the peacemakers, for they shall be called sons of God.	Gluttony

Prayer

Heavenly Father,
You are the Mighty Deliverer
and the eternal Prince of Peace.
Help us to speak the truth,
to defend goodness,
and to protect beauty.
Father, free us from all that hurts us.
Guide us in your ways of peace.
Save us from sin and darkness.
Draw close to us. Help us.
Deliver us.
Through Christ our Lord.
Amen.

Three Truths on Being Delivered by God:

+ God loves us and seeks to save us and deliver us from evil.
+ There is a false kingdom that is below our dignity and inheritance as God's children.
+ God gives us his guidance and grace to keep us within his kingdom of truth and goodness.

The Psalmist's Prayer

"You are a hiding place for me,
you preserve me from trouble;
you surround me with deliverance."

Psalm 32:7

Abundant Life

"I am the good shepherd. The good shepherd lays down his life for the sheep. He who is a hireling and not a shepherd, whose own the sheep are not, sees the wolf coming and leaves the sheep and flees; and the wolf snatches them and scatters them. He flees because he is a hireling and cares nothing for the sheep. I am the good shepherd; I know my own and my own know me, as the Father knows me and I know the Father; and I lay down my life for the sheep."

John 10:11–15

Prince and Savior

"The God of our fathers raised Jesus whom you killed by hanging him on a tree. God exalted him at his right hand as Leader and Savior, to give repentance to Israel and forgiveness of sins."

Acts 5:30–31

Embolism Prayer

Deliver us, Lord, we pray,

from every evil,

graciously grant peace in our days,

that,

by the help of your mercy,

we may be always free from sin

and safe from all distress,

as we await the blessed hope

and the coming of our Savior,

Jesus Christ.

Additional Reading:

If you'd like to know more about seeking and spreading God's kingdom, this book can help:

Jeffrey Kirby, *God's Search for Us: Five Lessons from a Missing Coin* (Pontifex University Press, 2018).

OUR DECISION

For thine is the kingdom, the power, and the glory, now and forever.

AMEN.

Can I Call You Dad?

In one of my previous parish assignments, I was pastorally involved with a couple in the process of an adoption. The child being adopted was a young teenager and had a life of untold disappointment and suffering. The social workers warned the couple that this adoption would be a massive labor of love. The husband and wife were eager, but they had no idea what they were getting into. The adoption went through and the young person arrived at their home.

Everything unraveled fast. Their new child provoked fights with neighbors, mistreated pets, snuck out at night, shoplifted from local stores, vandalized a park monument, skipped classes, harassed fellow students, was caught with stolen prescription drugs, yelled and screamed, hid behind locked doors and was unwilling to communicate. This behavior went on for almost a year, and every Sunday the faces of the new parents showed more exhaustion, distress, and anxiety. But they persevered. They addressed every act of defiance and misconduct. They spoke while they were being yelled at, and they loved while they were being mocked and betrayed.

As an effort to nurture constructive behavior, the father would invite his new child to join him for yard work, fix-up projects around the house, and errands around the community. The young person seemed disinterested and annoyed on every occasion. He refused to engage in conversation, but still the father tried and tried.

This back-and-forth continued without reprieve, yet the parents were committed. This was their child and they would give their absolute best. One year became almost two and things seemed to calm down a little. The child seemed more comfortable, leaving the bedroom door open and saying a few words at meals. There were fewer phone calls from the school and fewer neighbors banging on their door.

They told me the gradual progress reached a breakthrough one day while the father and child rode in the car. In the midst of a pleasant conversation, the child hesitantly asked, "Can I ask you something? It's a little weird."

"You can ask me anything you want. Is everything okay?"

The man told me later that a thousand things raced through his mind: Is this about drugs? A teenage pregnancy? Suicide? But he quieted his own soul and waited.

The child continued, "No, it's all right. I don't have any questions," and stared out the window.

The father let things sit for a few minutes and then said, "You know I love you. You can ask me whatever you want. I want to make sure you're safe."

The child looked at him, as if testing his sincerity, and

then said, "Well, I just wanted to ask . . . you know . . . if it would be okay . . . yeah, if it would be okay . . . ," and then the conversation seemed to get stuck.

The father was now very worried and increased his response, "Please, let me know what's on your heart. What's going on? You can say anything."

The child began to tear up and, with a crackling voice, asked, "Well . . . okay. If you're all right with it. . . . Well, is it okay . . . Can I call you Dad?"

Needless to say, after such an earth-shaking question, both father and child were shedding some tears. The man pulled his car over, got out, and embraced him as few people will ever experience. "Yes, yes, absolutely! Yes, call me Dad! You're my child. I love you! Yes, yes, yes!"

The drama didn't end after that breakthrough, but a confirmed identity and an established relationship helped them get through every struggle and difficulty.

Our Call

As we've walked through the Lord's Prayer, we should return to that powerful salutation, "Our Father." Like the child in that story, we are loved, cared for, forgiven, accepted, led, fed, delivered, and embraced by a father who has called us his own. And we, for our part, need to become comfortable in calling God our Father, our heavenly Dad. He's given us permission. He's called us his sons and daughters. Now, we need to trust him, open ourselves to him, follow his ways, and allow him to work in our souls. We have to let him be our Father. We have to welcome his fathering—his loving kindness— into our daily lives.

The Lord Jesus solemnly promised us, "If a man loves me, he will keep my word, and my Father will love him, and we will come to him and make our home with him" (Jn 14:23).

The divine family wants to make their home with us! God invites us to be with him. The Holy Trinity calls us to divine fellowship. We have been adopted and accepted by the living God. We are his sons and daughters. We are family. St. Paul explains, "And because you are sons, God has sent the Spirit of his Son into our hearts, crying, 'Abba! Father!' So through God you are no longer a slave but a son, and if a son than an heir" (Gal 4:6–7).

The Seven Tenets

In grasping the intimacy of God's call to us, we can more deeply appreciate the deep familiarity of the salutation of the Lord's Prayer, "Our Father." The greeting reminds us that the all-powerful and ever-living God, the Ancient of Days and Mighty Warrior, is truly our Father. We are his children, his kids. We are called to understand the dignity and glory that he has bestowed upon us. This is the foundation of our lives, and as such, it's the foundation of the various parts of the Lord's Prayer.

With an awareness of the salutation's boldness, we were able to walk through the seven tenets of the great prayer.

We started by going through the first portion of the Lord's Prayer. We dived into the glory of God's name, the splendor of his kingdom, and the utter graciousness of his holy will. After exploring these tenets, we moved into the last four petitions of the Lord's Prayer. These involved supplications and we dissected the biblical meaning of our requests to God for him to "give us," "forgive us," "lead us," and "deliver us."

In processing these seven tenets, we were able to see the depth and breadth of what the Lord Jesus is showing us and how he is teaching us to pray.

The Doxology

In the biblical account of the Lord's Prayer, contained principally in St. Matthew's Gospel (although St. Luke has an abbreviated version in his Gospel), the prayer concludes with the request for deliverance.

The Sacred Tradition of the Church, however, added a doxology—a three-part petition—to the end of the Lord's Prayer. The doxology was a devotional summation and evangelical declaration of the three main points of the prayer. It announces that the kingdom, the power, and the glory belong by right to our heavenly Father. The doxology is an adjusted version of the prayer that St. John heard in his mystical visit to the heavens: "And I heard every creature in heaven and on earth and under the earth and in the sea, and all therein, saying: 'To him who sits upon the throne and to the Lamb be blessing and honor and glory and might for ever and ever!'" (Rv 5:13).

While the doxology is not popularly used in personal prayer by Catholics, it does have a privileged placed in the communion rite of the Mass and is prayed by Catholics when united for public worship.

Father and Son

Having gone through a comprehensive summary of the various tenets of the Lord's Prayer, it's important for us to understand why the Lord Jesus gave this prayer to us. The apostles asked him, "Lord, teach us to pray," and his response was precisely this prayer. And he gave it to us for a reason. In addition to the salutation and the seven tenets of the prayer, therefore, we should also take some steps back and look at the mosaic formed by the Lord's Prayer.

Ultimately, every piece of it reveals and emphasizes the paradigm of father and son. It's an indication to us of the love and affection that God has for us as his children. He wishes to approach us and have communion with us as Father. This radical and absolutely good paradigm is in contrast to the master and slave paradigm born from fallen hearts in a fallen world.

In opposition to the self-knowledge that God gives us himself as Father, and to the constant overtures that he gives us to be members of his divine family, the master/slave paradigm distorts the image of God. It turns him into a monster and a tyrant. It makes him someone who desires to harm or humiliate us. As Pope St. John Paul II observed in his book *Crossing the Threshold of Hope,* "*Original sin attempts, then, to abolish fatherhood,* destroying its rays which permeate the created world, placing in doubt the truth about God who is Love and leaving man only with a sense of the master/slave relationship. . . . And consequently, man feels goaded to do battle against God. No differently than in any epoch of history, the enslaved man is driven to take sides against the master who keeps him enslaved" (p. 228).

And so, the choice is ours. We can succumb to our

fallenness and the lies of evil and approach God as the master who has to be overthrown, or we can see the revelation that he gives us and the love he shows us and accept his loving fatherhood. Will we live as beloved sons and daughters or rebellious, self-made slaves?

In his prayer, the Lord Jesus shows us the blessing of sonship. He unveils the path of sonship. He gives guidance for our lives and for our prayer, since we should always live as we pray.

What paradigm will we choose? What father will shepherd us in this life? Will we accept our vocation as the sons and daughters of God? Will we seek his kingdom?

Our Call and Commission

In the Upper Room, as the Lord Jesus initiated the definitive battle against the kingdom of evil by his passion, death, and resurrection, he said to the apostles, as he also says to us today: "As my Father appointed a kingdom for me, so do I appoint for you" (Lk 22:29).

This kingdom of light and goodness is the kingdom of our Father. He has entrusted it to us. It has been placed in our hearts and in our hands. By accepting our call to live as his children, and by being guided by the teachings of the Lord's Prayer, we are beckoned to pick up the mantle and live its way of love, share its truth and peace, fight for its victory over evil and darkness, and labor and suffer so that it can be spread and take root in every heart and in every part of our world.

The Lord Jesus tells us, "Peace be with you. As the Father has sent me, even so I send you" (Jn 20:21). This is the summons given to the sons and daughters of God.

Will we heed the commission? Will we continue the work of our Lord and older brother as he vanquishes evil and exalts goodness and holiness?

What will we decide?

Spiritual Matrix

TENET OF THE LORD'S PRAYER	GIFT OF THE HOLY SPIRIT	CORRESPONDING VIRTUE	BEATITUDE	CAPITAL SIN
Hallowed be thy name.	Fear of the Lord	Temperance	Blessed are the poor in spirit, for theirs is the kingdom of heaven.	Pride
Thy kingdom come.	Piety	Justice	Blessed are the meek, for they shall inherit the earth.	Wrath
Thy will be done on earth as it is in heaven.	Knowledge	Hope	Blessed are those who mourn, for they shall be comforted.	Envy
Give us this day our daily Bread.	Fortitude	Courage	Blessed are those who hunger and thirst for righteousness, for they shall be satisfied.	Sloth
Forgive us our trespasses as we forgive those who trespass against us.	Counsel	Prudence	Blessed are the merciful, for they shall obtain mercy.	Greed
And lead us not into Temptation.	Understanding	Faith	Blessed are the pure in heart, for they shall see God.	Lust
But deliver us from evil.	Wisdom	Charity	Blessed are the peacemakers, for they shall be called sons of God.	Gluttony

BIBLIOGRAPHY

General Reference

Catechism of the Catholic Church. Second Edition. Vatican City State: Libreria Editrice Vaticana, 1997.

Tertullian, Cyprian, and Origen on the Lord's Prayer. New York: Vladimir's Seminary Press, 2004.

Theme-Based References

Aquinas, Thomas. *Summa Theologica,* II-II, Q. 83. Translated by the Fathers of the English Dominican Province. Allen, Texas: Christian Classics, 1981 (Reprint).

Baker, Kenneth. *The Will of God: Finding and Fulfilling Your Purpose in Life.* San Francisco: Ignatius Press, 2012.

Beale, G. K. *We Become What We Worship: A Biblical Theology of Idolatry.* Downers Grove: IVP Academic, 2008.

Cantalamessa, Raniero. *Contemplating the Trinity.* Frederick, Maryland: The Word Among Us Press, 2007.

Eldredge, John. *Fathered by God*. Nashville: Thomas Nelson, 2009.

Hahn, Scott. *A Father Who Keeps his Promises*. Ann Arbor: Servant Publications, 1998.

———. *Understanding "Our Father."* With Patristic Appendixes on the Lord's Prayer. Steubenville: Emmaus Road Publishing, 2018.

John Paul II. *Crossing the Threshold of Hope*. Edited by Vittorio Messori. New York: Alfred Knopf, 1994.

Kirby, Jeffrey. *Be Not Troubled: A Personal 6-Day Retreat with Fr. Jean-Pierre DeCaussade*. Notre Dame: Ave Maria Press, 2019.

———. *Teach Us to Pray*. Charlotte: Saint Benedict Press, 2014.

Nouwen, Henri. *Can You Drink the Cup?* Notre Dame: Ave Maria Press, 2001.

———. *The Return of the Prodigal Son*. New York: Image Books, 1992.

———. *Wounded Healer*. New York: Image Books, 1972.

Packer, J. I. *Praying the Lord's Prayer*. Wheaton: Crossway, 2007.

Pennington, Jonathan. *The Sermon on the Mount and Human Flourishing*. Grand Rapids: Baker Academic, 2017.

Philippe, Jacques. *Called to Life*. New York: Scepter Press, 2008.

———. *Searching for and Maintaining Peace*. New York: Alba House, 2012.

————. *Thirsting for Prayer.* New York: Scepter Press, 2014.

Pitre, Brant. *Jesus and the Jewish Roots of the Eucharist.* New York: Doubleday, 2011.

Ratzinger, Joseph. *Jesus of Nazareth: From the Baptism in the Jordan to the Transfiguration.* Translated by Adrian Walker. New York: Doubleday, 2007.

Shea, John. *To Dare the Our Father: A Transformative Spiritual Practice.* Collegeville: Liturgical Press, 2018.

Von Balthasar, Hans Urs. *Prayer.* Translated by Graham Harrison. San Francisco: Ignatius Press, 1986.

Willimon, William and Stanley Hauerwas. *Lord, Teach Us: The Lord's Prayer and the Christian Life.* Nashville: Abington Press, 1996.

Wright, N.T. *The Lord and His Prayer.* Grand Rapids: Eerdmans Publishing, 1996.